JAMES
DUNN

JAMES DUNN

Champion for Religious Liberty

foreword by
BILL MOYERS

edited by
J. BRENT WALKER

SMYTH&HELWYS
PUBLISHING INCORPORATED   MACON, GEORGIA
WWW.HELWYS.COM

SMYTH&
HELWYS

Smyth & Helwys Publishing, Inc.
6316 Peake Road
Macon, Georgia 31210-3960
1-800-747-3016
© 1999 by Smyth & Helwys Publishing
All rights reserved.
Printed in the United States of America.

J. Brent Walker, editor

Proceeds from the sale of this book go to the Baptist Joint Committee Endowment.

Photos courtesy, Baptist Joint Committee, 200 Maryland Ave. NE, Washington DC 20002.
Cartoons courtesy, Joe McKeever and Doug Marlette.

J. Brent Walker, editor
     James Dunn: champion for religious liberty.
     pp. cm.
     (alk. paper)
     1. Dunn, James M., 1932–   .
     I. Walker, J. Brent.
     BX6495.D89J46   1999
     286'.1'092—dc21   99-39706
                                                                    CIP

ISBN 1-57312-295-5

Contents

Foreword

Bill Moyers

FOR SEVERAL YEARS after leaving Washington, D.C., for New York, I lived in the township where Hezekiah Smith was born in 1737. Smith went forth from there to preach the Word in the vast spiritual precincts of the South, traveling 4,235 bruising miles on horseback. From his labors came one of the first Baptist missionary societies and—because Baptists believed in the life of the mind and the power of the spirit—the founding of Brown University.

Baptists also believed in freedom. Hezekiah Smith volunteered in Washington's army. In fact, six of Washington's twenty-one brigade chaplains were Baptists, each of whom had grieved at having been taxed by colonial governments to support the established church. We have it on the authority of Washington himself that "Baptists were throughout America uniformly and almost unanimously the firm friends to civil liberty . . . and our glorious revolution."

When I think of Hezekiah Smith, I think of James Dunn.

Recently I drove through Groton, Connecticut, where Valentine Wightman organized a Baptist church in 1705 when the fine for forming "separate companies of worship in private houses" was ten shillings "for every such offence."

When I think of Valentine Wightman, I think of James Dunn.

On a vacation in Maine, I stood where a Baptist church was organized in 1641 by William Screven. In that church, Screven exercised his conscience on the issue of baptism, for which he was imprisoned and fined. Under constant harassment of government and religious authorities, he finally led his little congregation of seventeen souls all the way to South Carolina in search of liberty.

When I think of William Screven, I think of James Dunn.

On another trip to New England, I drove through Lynn, Massachusetts. There, in 1751, Obadiah Holmes was given thirty stripes with a three-corded whip after he violated the colonial law against taking communion with another Baptist. Baptists were only a "pitiful negligible minority" in Massachusetts, but they were denounced as "the incendiaries of the Commonwealth and the infectors of persons in matters of religion." For refusing to pay tribute to the official state religion they were fined, flogged, and exiled. Holmes refused the offer of friends to pay his fine so that he could be released. He refused the strong drink they said would anesthetize the pain. Sober, he endured the ordeal; sober still, he would one day write: "It is the love of liberty that must free the soul."

When I think of Obadiah Holmes, I think of James Dunn.

James Dunn belongs to a long train of Baptists who have struggled—and often suffered—for a free church in a free state. Freedom is the bedrock of our faith. In the words of the Baptist scholar Walter Rauschenbusch, "The Christian faith, as Baptists hold it, sets spiritual experience boldly to the front as the one great thing in religion." That experience is unique to each of us. God moves in mysterious ways, and the mystery is made manifest one by one.

At the core of our faith is what we call "soul competency," the competence of the individual before God. Created with the imprint of divinity, from the mixed clay of earth, we are endowed with the capacity to choose, to be what James Dunn calls "response-able," a grown-up before God.

At last count there were twenty-seven varietites of Baptists in America. My particular crowd holds that while the Bible is our anchor, it is no icon; that revelation continues; that truth is not frozen in doctrine but emerges from experience and encounter; that the City of God is a past, present, and future community whose inhabitants are not all alike and may even surprise us in being counted among the faithful. In Jesus Christ we see the power of the Living Word over tired practice and dead belief. In his relationship with women, the sick, the outcast, and the stranger—even with the hated tax collector—Jesus broke new ground. The literal observance of the law was not to quench the spirit of justice. "The sabbath was made for humankind, and not humankind for the sabbath" (Mark 2:27).

These beliefs do not make for lawless anarchy or the religion of lone rangers. They do not mean we can float safely on the little raft of our own faith while the community flounders. They are the ground of personhood. They aim for a community with moral integrity (despite our fallenness as human beings), the wholeness that flows from mutual obligation. Our religion is an adventure in freedom within boundaries of accountability.

Essential to our faith is a free church in a free state. No government can be permitted to compromise any soul's exercise of freedom. For any government to say, "This experience is more to be preferred by the state than that one," is the slippery slope to the subversion of faith. Accordingly, the separation of church and state becomes the first line of defense in protecting that "one great thing in religion" against coercion. Every generation must take up the challenge because the threat to religious liberty is as perennial as the seasons.

The threat has come in our time not from a direct assault by government; it has come from within the Christian community. In the past twenty years, fundamentalist Baptists have forged an alliance to take over a major political party and to promote an agenda of state-sanctioned prayer, public subsidies, and government privileges. Their first, and most successful, strategy was to seize control of the Southern Baptist Convention, whose pews they intended to turn into precincts of power.

It was a remarkable coup, made possible by exploiting an unsuspecting laity's respect for the Bible. Most Baptists grow up believing the Bible to be the sufficient authority for our faith and practice; its witness to revelation we take as the starting point for our own spiritual growth over a lifetime of attempting to learn and to apply what the Scriptures tell us. There is always incipient in this belief the danger of idolatry, of exalting the Bible as holy instead of the God whose spirit moves within it. Rauschenbusch, among others, warned against Baptists who would "use the Bible just as other denominations use their creed." He feared that just as in Catholicism only priests could consecrate the sacraments and forgive sins, so among Baptists an elect would declare: "You must believe everything which we think the Bible means and says." They would impose on everyone else "their little interpretation of the great Book as the creed to which all good Baptists must cleave."

Incredibly, this is what happened. The cabal that took over the Southern Baptist Convention could only maintain their hold if they were the undisputed masters of doctrine. But Baptists have no doctrine to control, given our conviction that personal experience —that "one great thing"—makes each of us responsible for understanding God's will in our lives. But what if the conspirators substituted the Bible itself for the "one great thing" and then asserted the primacy of their biblical interpretation over the validity of personal spiritual experience? Individual men and women would no longer have to bother plumbing the meaning of the text; an ecclesiastical imperium would do it for them. Churches whose polity had been Christian democracy would take a radical turn. The laity would be subjugated to the preacher and the preacher to the denominational politburo, which alone would decide who is, and who isn't, a true Baptist. With the dissidents excluded, who would protest any erosion of the wall between church and state? The entire apparatus could be safely aligned with political operatives who slickly promised the restoration of a "Christian America."

James Dunn saw the implications immediately. As head of the Baptist Joint Committee on Public Affairs (BJC) in Washington, D.C., his charge was to identify and to resist just such alliances between church and state; he was to be the watchdog that barked when either church or state entered the other's backyard. A cause to bark surfaced in the 1980s. A BJC staffer had learned that a resolution passed by the Southern Baptist Convention in 1982, calling for a constitutional amendment in support of school prayer, had actually been drafted by a White House assistant. James pronounced the action to be "the most glaring illustration of the successful attempt of secular politics to move into the denomination." There were other examples as the clique in command of the Convention launched a series of stealth moves to align the organization to partisan causes. It was a painful thing for James Dunn to sound the trumpet against his own denomination; he had spent his whole life in the Southern Baptist Convention and was himself a theological conservative. But as a matter of conscience, he felt obliged to declare that the new order's political designs would undermine the wall that separates church and state.

When he spoke out, they tried to silence him. When he would not be silenced, they tried to fire him, as they had summarily and even cruelly purged other denominational employees who would not bow to the new orthodoxy. Fortunately, Dunn's own BJC board, which in addition to the Southern Baptist Convention includes representatives from eight other Baptist denominations, refused to abandon him. The Convention hierarchy then cut his budget. He went out and raised funds to make up the loss. Not only could the watchdog bark, but he could also bite, and the poachers of the First Amendment soon found the seats of their pants in shreds.

The Lenin of the SBC—the man who plotted and perpetrated the takeover—had determined that fundamentalists would be named to run every one of the denomination's seminaries, colleges, boards, and agencies. But he had more than religious power in mind. It turned out that he belonged to a secret organization of right-wing ideologues and political activists—the Council on National Policy—who met regularly to coordinate their agenda with religious allies. Its members included Senator Jesse Helms, Oliver North, Jerry Falwell, Joseph Coors, and Phyllis Schlafly, among others. I inadvertently stumbled on this fellow's membership while reporting for a documentary series on "God and Politics." When I pressed him on camera about his association with the organization, he grew indignant and broke off the interview.

By this time he held the executive committee of the Southern Baptist Convention under his thumb, and he demanded that it pass a resolution censuring me. His crowd also went after the corporate sponsor of my television series, which was pressured to withdraw its support of my work. But there was little they could do to an independent journalist.

James Dunn was another matter—or so they thought—and their full wrath fell on him. His new heresy, in their sight, was to appear in the documentary and to talk about soul freedom. He told me in the interview,

> Freedom of conscience is not simply the popular kind of man on the street understanding of freedom of conscience, but freedom of conscience as an innate, inherent, universal right for every human being. . . . The right to say no to God, the right to say no to any and all assaults on the intellect. The right to say no to any and all appeals to the imagination and emotions. The insistence upon bowing the knee to no man—that's been right at the heart of whatever makes Baptists different.

Those views riled the fundamentalists, who wanted no challenge to the blanket of conformity they were pulling across the Southern Baptist Convention. And they were further enraged that he would go on national television to sound the alarm! The man was clearly dangerous—an incendiary of the Commonwealth—and since fundamentalists were no longer permitted to flog dissenters, they would have to resort to other measures to rid their theocracy of him.

At first they attempted to smear him, but this proved hard to do to a man who doesn't cuss, smoke, drink, or think harshly even of Methodists. They did succeed in defunding the BJC, cutting off its every last dime of financial support from the Southern Baptist

Convention. Rarely have I witnessed such courage and persever-
ance as were then exhibited by James Dunn, his staff, and their
board. As you'll read later in this book, he and the BJC survived to
fight another day, and another, and another, subsequently winning
some of their most important victories in the continuing battle for
religious liberty.

What is his secret? He believes in a very big God. As
Rauschenbusch once wrote,

> Little beliefs make little men . . . It is possible to play 'Nearer, My
> God to Thee' with one finger on a little reed organ of four
> octaves. But it is very different music when the same melody is
> played with all the resources of a great pipe organ and in all the
> richness of full harmony.

James Dunn pulls out all the stops and pumps with all his might.
Watching him in action, I am reminded that God sends messengers
in odd shapes and sizes and from unexpected places. Who would
have thought that one of the most effective advocates of religious
freedom in our time would grow up on the east side of a Texas
cowtown, sound like a horse-trader, and dress like a trail-driver?
Who would ever have imagined that such an unassuming figure
would become one of the most effective champions of social justice
and Christian morality in the last quarter of the twentieth century?

Sometimes in my mind's eye I see him toting a Bible in one
hand and a voting tally in another. From one he draws his principles and from the other his prowess. "I don't want a man up there
who can't count votes," Lyndon Johnson once said as he marched
his staff up to Congress on the day a key bill hung in the balance.
James Dunn can count. He can also sniff, and sniffing is the art of
the bloodhound.

Baptists have never had a more savvy master of the legislative
process, where the most offensive infringement of religious liberty
can be inflicted in fine print that no one else bothers to read until
it is too late. A lesser man would have been blindsided by the likes

of Pat Robertson and his former chief lieutenant, Ralph Reed, who once boasted that the Religious Right had "learned how to move under radar in the cover of the night with shrubbery strapped to our helmets." Yes, but just when they were about to make off with the First Amendment, James Dunn hove into sight; the man sees with his eyes closed. The back room boys learned long ago that they couldn't blow smoke in his eyes; he earned their respect for his shrewdness, integrity, and utter lack of self-aggrandizement. With his instincts and talents he could have become an influential lobbyist, raking in huge fees from powerful interests. But James Dunn chose a different course.

He was chosen, rather. Let there be no doubt about this. Like his mentors, J. M. Dawson and T. B. Maston, the mystery of the Christ event has been central to James' understanding of his faith and practice. He had his encounter early on, and it transformed him, producing a life devoted to his principles and aware at every turn of that transcendent presence. People like James Dunn were described quite neatly in H. Wheeler Robinson's profile of the Baptist tradition:

> Nothing atones for the absence of those memories of childhood and youth which are progressively hallowed by the faith of the adult and gain a richer interpretation by the experience of life. The familiar walls of the church, the familiar phrases of prayer and praise, gain a sacramental quality, so as to be inseparable in memory from the experience they mediated. They have helped to bring us into a living tradition, so that we might discover "how great a thing it is" to live at the end of so many ages.

You will learn in these pages how James Dunn arrived into that living tradition. You will learn how this clarinet-playing, foot-tapping, hymn-singing good ol' boy earned his place in that cloud of witnesses that includes Hezekiah Smith, Valentine Wightman, William Screven, Walter Rauschenbusch, J. M. Dawson, T. B. Maston, and so many others; how he found in his beloved Marilyn a soul mate; and how he refused to quit at one Thermopylae after another. These tributes are, of course, written by friends; his capacity to inspire deep, sustaining friendships is an unforgettable mark of the man.

My own life has been indelibly touched by James Dunn. Through thick and thin he has been my friend. Almost half a century ago, Marilyn, then his fiancee, was critically injured in a car accident near my hometown of Marshall, Texas. James rushed from Forth Worth to be at her side. My mother, Ruby, just happened to be at the hospital where he waited for news of Marilyn's condition. He was a stranger, and when my mother heard what had happened, she introduced herself to him, learned he was from Southwestern Seminary, and insisted that he make our home his home until the crisis passed. He never forgot her.

Ruby Moyers died recently at the age of ninety-one. James was scheduled to speak that weekend—as he does practically every weekend—at some distant church on behalf of religious liberty (what else?). I assumed he would not—could not—make it to the funeral. But I looked up, and there he was. In the funeral parlor he joined in the family circle as nieces and nephews, grandchildren and cousins, recalled their own experiences with my mother. Then, during the service at Central Baptist Church, he recounted his first meeting with her and spoke movingly of her kindness to him. And then he was gone—to catch one more plane to one more city for one more testimony to one more Baptist church whose congregation he would summon to remembrance of that "one great thing."

Who would not cherish such a brother?

Bill Moyers and James Dunn at Riverside Church, New York City, 1995

Preface

———— *J. Brent Walker* ————

THIS BOOK IS ABOUT THE LIFE AND WORK of James M. Dunn. In a sense, it's premature because neither is yet finished. James will begin teaching at the new divinity school at Wake Forest University in September 1999 and will serve as president of the Baptist Joint Committee Foundation—hopefully to raise a pile of money for the agency he has so ably led for almost two decades. So, he's definitely not retiring. "Who would retire by taking two jobs instead of one?" James has mused.

But the occasion of James' stepping aside as executive director of the Baptist Joint Committee provides a propitious moment to reflect on the life of this extraordinary Baptist and champion for religious liberty. At least Mark McElroy at Smyth & Helwys Publishing thought so. And when he asked me to serve as general editor of this volume, I was flattered and quickly agreed.

In honoring the life and work of James Dunn, this book was never intended to be, nor is it, a formal *festschrift*. True, James earned a doctorate in Christian Social Ethics from Southwestern Seminary and did postdoctoral work at the London School of Economics in economics and political science. But academic life could never fully hold James—the inveterate activist, the peripatetic doer, the street-fighting sage, and the closest thing to a bishop we nonhierarchical, freedom-loving Baptists can find. Instead, this volume represents a warm, from-the-heart remembrance of James Dunn from the pen of thirteen people who know him well—"cronies," as James would say.

James could never be contained by his own state of Texas, as big and broad a place as it is. Still more of a "Texican" than a Washingtonian, James cannot be understood and appreciated without reference to both. So we endeavored to balance the chapters about his first forty-eight years in Texas—recounted by Foy Valentine, John Newport, and Marvin Griffin—with those by folks who have known him primarily in Washington for nearly twenty years. Mike Smith chronicles Dunn's crossing the Potomac, and the likes of Senator Mark Hatfield, Tony Campolo, and James' pastor, Lynn Bergfalk, pick up the story.

Moreover, James' work at the Baptist Joint Committee cried out to be chronicled from the inside. Accordingly, three chapters are written by former BJC colleagues: Victor Tupitza (1979–1990), Buzz Thomas (1985–1993), and Pam Parry (1991–1996).

James' influence extended way beyond Baptist life along the Dallas/Forth Worth/Washington, D.C. axis. Without compromising his "Baptistness" one bit, James has always been an "ecumaniac" in the best sense of the word. Rabbi James Rudin, the only non-Baptist contributor to the book, honors James from the perspective of the interreligious community.

Walter Shurden, the quintessential interpreter of Baptist history for the lay reader as well as the scholar, places James' ministry in historical context, comparing his life with that of Elder John Leland.

Each author brings something a little different. I have tried not to edit them too much, allowing their own style, tenor, flavor, and idiom to come through. One commercial: do not dare skip over the foreword, as I sometimes do. Bill Moyers, a close friend of James from college days, writes a touching remembrance that will tug at your heartstrings and bring tears to your eyes.

Yes, only friends and cronies were asked to contribute to this book. This has resulted in lavish, but not undeserved, praise that, quite frankly, made James blush when he sneaked a peek at as he reviewed some of the chapters. None of his many detractors were invited to contribute. Hey, they've had ample opportunity to beat up on James for many years. But I suspect that, had they been asked, most would grudgingly own up to admiration or even appreciation for the life and work of this truly remarkable Baptist.

So read, enjoy, learn, laugh, and celebrate this extraordinary liberty-loving, freedom-fighting Baptist. Many thanks to the good people at Smyth & Helwys for their vision and cooperation in getting this project going. A special thanks to my assistant, Holly Shaver, whose literary, organizational, and computer skills were indispensable to this book's timely completion.

Brent Walker and James Dunn at the U.S. Capitol, 1995

Unus and Unicus

Foy Valentine

UNUS AND UNICUS. ONE AND UNIQUE. This is James Dunn. Singular and without an equal. What more can be said? Much, much more. And thereby hangs this tale.

I first met James Dunn when he was a boy in Fort Worth, Texas. I was enrolled as a student at Southwestern Baptist Theological Seminary, and my only brother was his leader in a young people's Baptist Training Union at Evans Avenue Baptist Church. Even then James Dunn was awash in energy, alive with ideas, smart enough to hear grass grow, alert to all things bright and beautiful, tuned in to everything around him, and ethically concerned about what was happening in the world.

When he enrolled as a graduate student at Southwestern Seminary after college, it was absolutely natural for him to gravitate to the Christian ethics gangs. Those interest groups of concentrated benignity related to social concerns had formed because of the social climate of those times, the late 1940s and the early 1950s. They had formed because of the powerful presence of T. B. Maston, Professor of Christian Social Ethics at Southwestern. And they had formed because of the demands of the gospel of God in Christ, demands that were being brought into clear focus "in the fullness of time." With these young "troublers of Israel"—of whom I was one—James Dunn found immediate and lifelong kindred spirits.

After a high-voltage stint of Bible-chair teaching and Baptist student work at West Texas State University in Canyon, Texas, James Dunn became the associate director of the Texas Baptist Christian Life Commission where Jimmy Allen was the Director. There he began to hit his stride in the race to help Christians apply Christian principles in society at large and in daily living in particular. When the First Baptist Church of San Antonio called Allen as pastor, Dunn was called to run the Texas Baptist Christian Life Commission. And run it he did, with a vengeance, for some thirteen years before he was enlisted to direct the work of the Baptist Joint Committee on Public Affairs in Washington, D.C.

James Dunn was made for the Baptist Joint Committee, and the Baptist Joint Committee was made for James Dunn. The coming together of these two raging torrents has made history. In this confluence Dunn's lifework has been unfolding for two decades. It seems manifestly destined to continue to unfold, to blossom, and to bear important fruit far into the future.

A look at the qualities that have characterized Dunn's life and work as director of this nationally and internationally influential organization yields further insights into the reasons for his remarkable effectiveness.

Dunn is an authentic Christian. The faith in God that he embraced when he was quite young brought him once and for all under the lordship of Jesus Christ. He seems to have understood all along that as God's grace had persuaded him to bow his own knee to Jesus Christ as Lord, so God put no limits, and would allow none, in the long haul, on the ultimate goal that "every knee should bow" to the will of God, for persons, for institutions, for structures, for systems, and for principalities and powers. That genuine faith in God through Jesus Christ has been demonstrated in his faithful churchmanship, in his attention to his own Christian home, in his tirelessly peripatetic preaching in the United States and abroad, in season and out of season, and his nonstop counseling with innumerable young people who have been attracted to him and his high-voltage ministry. That faith informs and enlightens his daily life, his work, his writing, his speaking, his interviews, his steward- ship, and his politics. To his credit, he does not take his faith lightly or wear his religion on his sleeve. He does not enter glibly into "God-talk" or trivialize his faith by taking God's name in vain. What really makes James Dunn tick? His religion makes him tick.

James Dunn is a principled man. In the broadest sense of the word, he is a person who everlastingly tries to do the right thing in all situations, whether or not anyone is looking and no matter what the cost. It would not be appropriate to dwell on the abstract when talking about James; rather, the specific, concrete, principle of reli- gious liberty is the focal point of his life and work. This principle is where he elected to pitch his tent. Predecessors, like Lot, had viewed the pleasant pastures and well-watered plains where many other worthy causes and important principles could be engaged, but James, like Abraham, drove his scrawny flock to the rocky hill- sides. On those rocky hillsides he has unfalteringly, unswervingly, unflinchingly remained in stalwart support of religious liberty and its magnificent corollary—the separation of church and state. That principle, which long ago became the cornerstone of our American liberties, was once a despised and rejected notion. James Dunn helped to pump life into it. It has been often under heavy fire from big guns, possibly never more so than now. But it has been good to know, as Robert E. Lee said of Thomas Jonathan "Stonewall" Jackson, that when the shells were bursting, and the thunderstorms were raging, and the lightning was flashing, we could always see James Dunn standing like a stone wall.

James Dunn's life has been peculiarly marked by friendships. These friendships have not been run of the mill, casual, or transi- tory. On the contrary, his friendships have tended to be covenantal. They have run profoundly deep. They have elicited sacrifice. They have demonstrated self-giving love. They have endured across the years, indeed across many decades. They have forged the steel around which the superstructure of his Baptist Joint Committee has been built. Before that they helped pour the concrete on which the superstructure could be built. These friendships, these warmly personal relationships, have been the stuff out of which James Dunn's incredibly wide-ranging connections could be fashioned into an enduring network in support of the separation of church and state. When the fundamentalists in control of the Southern Baptist Convention sought to get rid of James Dunn by cutting off all their funding of the Baptist Joint Committee, they might as well have targeted Robin Hood in the middle of Sherwood Forest. Every tree, squirrel, bird, and fox was ready to come to his rescue. So now he and his agency stand stronger, healthier, and more financially secure than ever before. Long live these friends.

James Dunn is a man of courage. He is not really foolhardy, but he is about as far from being what fire-eating preachers used to call a "pusillanimous pussy footer" as anybody you would ever in this world want to meet. He is the sort of person you would hope to have around if you ever got in a really tough fight. He is the sort of companion you would want with you on a dark night when you met the devil face to face in the middle of the road—who, when you were getting ready to run, you could count on to spit in the devil's eye.

America, in its relatively brief history, has produced a goodly crop of courageous men and women. There are good reasons for this. Our forebears were a hardy lot, or they would never have pulled up stake and trudged, walked, ran, swum, rafted, sailed, or crawled to this untamed wilderness, to this brave new world, to this impossible dream, to this raw land of beginning again. To do what James Dunn has done with his life and work, you have to have the right stuff, a sizable part of which is raw courage, the courage to "fight with beasts of Ephesus" as Paul did or to stand up for the separation of church and state when the world around you is caving in for Caesar's mess of pottage. Salute the man for his nerve. Honor him for his courage. May his tribe increase.

James Dunn has tough skin. He would have been in big trouble all along if he had believed the bad things a lot of people were saying about him. He understood that just because *they* believed those things, he neither had to believe them nor be bothered by them. He knew that he could not be in the position to which God, and Baptists, had called him and have all men think well of him. In fact, he always kept this little morsel of truth in the back of his mind: "Woe unto you when all men shall think well of you." Right on, Jesus. Of course, a body who develops a tough skin can also let callouses form on his soul. The temptation of a person in the public glare, targeted often for opposition and abuse, railed at by foes and sometimes castigated by friends, is to become so hardened to opposition that the heart itself turns to stone. It is a temptation that, by the grace of God, James Dunn has avoided. While his skin is tough, his heart is remarkably tender. From his eye there often flows a sympathizing tear. His staff and friends, and sometimes perfect strangers, encounter his compassion. Still, his tough skin has been the gift of God, for without it he would have been forced long ago to throw in the towel, abandon the crusade, give up the fight. We respect his tough skin.

Loyalty is one of James Dunn's distinguishing personal qualities, and what a worthy characteristic it is. Disloyalty signals baseness, infidelity, and treachery—the very antitheses of what the ancient Greeks and Romans envisioned when they incorporated the warp and woof of their four cardinal virtues: (1) obligations assumed are obligations faithfully discharged; (2) commitments made are commitments kept; (3) debts incurred are debts honorably discharged; and (4) a word given is a word kept. James Dunn's loyalties have been a hallmark of his life. Constant in season and out of season, he has maintained faithful allegiance to his Lord, his Baptist heritage, his family ties, his raising, his teachers, and his numerous friends and allies in the crusade to maintain religious liberty and strengthen the separation of church and state. His steadfast loyalty, based not only on the truth for which he has sought to live, but also in the heartfelt attachment to the friends and supporters of that truth, signals the greatness of a noble spirit.

James Dunn has a remarkably high energy level. It may well be, of course, that he gets no stars in his crown for this. Maybe he was born that way. At least he has been that way for the half century I have known him. But at any rate, his high energy level, capacity for hard work, and enthusiasm for the labor his hands find every day have produced an impressive array of achievements in areas of public life that are important to us all. Instead of channeling that energy into areas of self-indulgence or the pursuit of pleasure or unworthy endeavors, it is to Dunn's everlasting credit that he has focused his energies on his special high calling from God in Christ Jesus. With laser beam intensity, he has kept his energy directed toward the goals for which the Baptist Joint Committee was established and for which his friends want it to continue to stand. Without Dunn's remarkable enthusiasm, there is no way his agency could have made the impact that has astounded observers over the years. Okay, so he has always worn out his suits from the inside. No matter. That energy focused for religious liberty and the separation of church and state has helped make a huge difference in our churches, in our nation, and in our world.

James Dunn is a generous man. I suppose most people do not know that James and Marilyn, his lovely and talented wife of almost fifty years, have been faithful and generous contributors to a wide variety of truly worthy causes. They have chosen a rigorously austere lifestyle in which things have been intentionally relegated to the backseat while persons and causes and important programs have been intentionally supported, aggrandized, and undergirded. It is good for us to look around and see that this champion of religious liberty is big enough to have extended his own stewardship beyond his immediate bailiwick to a larger world of need and challenge. It is the mark of a big man.

James Dunn is a truly patriotic American. It has been often observed that the relationship of church and state is the most important subject in the history of the West. To say, then, that James Dunn is a patriotic American is to say that his lifetime of labors in the vineyard of religious liberty and church-state separation has been a lifetime spent in helping America, in underpinning its very foundation, and in ensuring its continued vitality.

James Dunn is—I choose the word for this idea very carefully lest I elicit a guffaw—meek (humble, teachable, unassuming). About as much as anyone I know, he has steadfastly resisted standing on ceremony. His staff is far more likely to call him James than Dr. Dunn. At least he has never presumed to be a big dog, a big shot, or a big enchilada. Instead, he is always ready to write his own letters, make his own phone calls, sort the mail, run off his own copies, carry out his own load of pamphlets, speak to some faraway associational meeting (greater love than this hath no man—and very few women), stay up late to meet the deadline over which others too are still sweating, and generally to bear more than his full share of the grunt work that inevitably is the prelude to the kind of success that has distinguished his life and work.

A grateful recipient of a goodly heritage from his parents, teachers, and heroes, particularly T. B. Maston and J. M. Dawson, on whose broad shoulders he has rested and is still resting, James Dunn stands out now like Venus on a summer evening. Such gratitude separates the men from the boys, exudes honor, demonstrates character, and signals order in the soul. Those who join here in his parade honor not only the man, but also the great cause to which he has joyfully and successfully given his life.

So I join in saluting, with all the smartness I can muster, James Dunn, *Unus and unicus.*

(From left) James Dunn, Jimmy Allen, Foy Valentine, and A. C. Miller at First Baptist Church, Houston TX, 1972

The Down-Home Prophet
———— *Tony Campolo* ————

WHEN I FIRST MET JAMES DUNN, I could not figure him out. He talked like a hillbilly preacher, and yet the things he said revealed the mind of a sophisticated social critic. As the years unfolded, I realized that both of these impressions were valid. He possesses a preaching style that would make him welcome among the simplest people in America. Farmers and factory workers relate to him with ease, while erudite scholars find him intellectually challenging. But what most characterizes him in my mind is that he is an articulate spokesperson for basic Baptist principles, especially as they relate to the relationship between church and state.

He preaches an evangelical version of the gospel, but he is hardly the darling of fundamentalists. As I have gotten to know him, I have realized that it is not the theological beliefs of fundamentalism that tick him off as much as it is the tactics of some of his fundamentalist opponents. He is a fair man, and when religious leaders use unfair tactics tinged with meanness, he goes ballistic. There is nothing calm about this man who knows how to pound the table and thunder forth as a biblical prophet. He is a loving man, and his love evokes a strong reaction whenever he sees people victimized by those who have power.

The Baptist Joint Committee, which he faithfully has led for so many years, has served as a voice in that strange political arena called Washington, D.C. He is well known on Capitol Hill and has

spoken out on behalf of the poor and the oppressed whenever their rights were being violated or they were being shortchanged when it came to justice. He knows how to get into the offices of congressmen and senators. Presidents have come to know him on a first name basis. Whenever our lawmakers want to know what Baptists think about anything, James Dunn is the one they turn to for answers.

Baptists come in many shapes and forms. Being committed to the doctrine of "soul competency," they hold a variety of opinions. It is often said that whenever two or three Baptists are gathered together, there are likely to be five or six opinions. For one spokesperson to articulate Baptists' perspectives to those who hold political power is a task both heavy and unenviable, but James Dunn has done it well.

Being a Baptist, Dunn has been strongly committed to the doctrine of separation of church and state. He therefore supports the Supreme Court's decision to remove state-sponsored prayer and Bible reading from public schools. This stand did not go over well with many Southern Baptist colleagues who believed that the removal of these religious exercises would lead to a spiritual disaster for the nation. James, however, felt that something was unfair about using tax dollars paid by nonreligious persons to support religious activities. So when the Supreme Court said this would no longer be allowed, he hailed the decision with enthusiasm.

It was James' belief that parents who wanted their children to hear the Bible read every day should do so at home. They should not expect the school to lead in a religious exercise. To his way of thinking, if parents believe their children should have Scripture and prayer every day, then they should provide the same and not be angry with the school system that refuses to do so on their behalf.

In reality, James is not opposed to discussing God in the classroom. He is not even opposed to Scripture being read in the public school system. He is, however, opposed to the expectation that employees of the state or of the local school board should lead in these practices. When Bill Clinton endorsed federal guidelines that clearly allowed for Bible reading and religious gatherings in public schools, *providing that the students themselves conduct such religious activities*, James thought this was a brilliant step in the right direction. It allowed religion in the public school, but not at the taxpayers' expense or in a manner that signaled state endorsement. Atheists would have nothing to complain about if students acted alone to conduct religious activities, because they simply would be exercising their First Amendment rights of freedom of religion and speech.

Of course, this allowance of religious gatherings in public schools would open the door for people of other religions to have the opportunity to express what they believe by reading from their scriptures. Muslims would be able to share readings from the Koran. Hindu students would be permitted to read from the Rig-Veda. That would be well and good as far as James was concerned. He is the kind of guy who believes that it would behoove Christians to learn about other religions. It would make for better understanding if all of us heard from scriptures and traditions other than our own.

To those who would advocate reading the Christian scriptures when the student body is mostly Baptist, Dunn would say, "What about Utah, where the majority of people are Mormons? Should Baptist children be subjected to daily readings from the Book of Mormon simply because the majority of the students are of the Mormon faith? And what about Hawaii, where the majority of students in some schools are Buddhist? Should Christians be subjected to readings by teachers from the Buddhist scriptures?"

Fair is fair, according to James Dunn. He does not want to see imposed on others the kind of oppressive religious indoctrination that Christians would not want to endure were they the minority. There is a big difference in his mind between tax-paid teachers reading Christian scriptures in accord with the requirement of law and students sharing freely their convictions in discussions. Unfortunately, Dunn's own Southern Baptist Convention did not agree with him on this issue. Differences on this matter soon reached a boiling point with the SBC saying it could no longer be part of the Baptist Joint Committee if James Dunn remained its primary spokesperson. The resulting SBC exodus was inevitable.

James is also adamantly opposed to school vouchers. This stand has set him over against not only the conservative wing of the Southern Baptist Convention, but also against some of his close friends who might be seen as representative of the religious left. As a case in point, Ron Sider, spokesperson for Evangelicals for Social Action (ESA), has strongly supported school vouchers as a means of improving the quality of education among the poor. It has been ESA's contention that vouchers will require public schools to be competitive with private and parochial schools. It can be argued that public schools tend to be top-heavy with administration that drains dollars from the classroom. Furthermore, ESA contends that because of their virtual monopoly on public funds for education, public schools have become lackadaisical and have tolerated incompetence in teaching. If parents get vouchers for their children, they can assign their tax dollars to either a public school or a parochial/private school. Soon the public schools of the country will have to respond with dramatic improvements. Furthermore, vouchers would allow poor families to have a choice of where their children attend school, as do wealthy families.

This kind of talk raises James' ire. He contends that vouchers would decimate the public school system. First of all, he argues, there would be a loss of necessary funding for public schools, which he believes are already in desperate financial straits. This loss of funds would further hurt the quality of public education. What is worse, many caring parents would use vouchers as a means of getting their children out of the public schools, while uncaring parents would not go through the trouble required to make the change.

James is also concerned that vouchers would allow private and parochial schools to choose the students they want while leaving the "problem" children in the public schools. Private schools are less likely to make the necessary expenditures for children with special needs, thereby leaving their expensive care to the public school system at the time when funds are being drained from it.

Perhaps the most insightful concern James Dunn has about vouchers stems from his historical awareness of why the public school system was created in the first place. In reality, public education was an attempt to facilitate the great "melting pot." Those persons who created public education realized that ours was a polyglot nation made of people from different religions and representing ethnic groups with diverse values. Through public education, children with varied backgrounds can get to know and appreciate each other and can create a common value system and unified worldview. Every sociologist knows that unless there is some instrument for people in a society to create a consensus for values and to grow into a common worldview, the possibilities of communal harmony are slight. If there are vouchers, questions Dunn, will not every weird group in America end up creating its own school? What would prevent the KKK from developing schools of its own? Could not the taxpayers find themselves financing the education of bigots?

To further support this argument against vouchers, allow me to point out that when I was in Northern Ireland, I asked both Catholic and Protestant leaders what could be done to end the religious strife of that war-torn part of the world. Their answer was to end a system of education that keeps Protestants and Catholics apart from each other. In Northern Ireland, there is something akin to our hypothetical voucher system. The result is that Protestant kids go to Protestant schools and Catholic kids go to Catholic school, and never do the twain meet. Even though Belfast is a relatively small city, very few Catholic teenagers have friends in the Protestant community, and vice versa. The implication of this situation for the reinforcement of negative stereotypes on both sides is all too obvious.

The concerns of James Dunn go far deeper than the separation of church and state. He does his best to provide a Baptist voice on behalf of the poor and oppressed people of the world. When the resources of the richest nation on the face of the earth should be employed to feed the needy and starving people of Asia or Africa, James' voice is heard on Capitol Hill. When the rights of people are violated because of their race, gender, or sexual orientation, you can count on James Dunn to raise his voice against such injustices. He believes Baptists should be ready to be a voice for those oppressed people who have no voice, and he himself is more than ready to identify in love with those who stand for equality. It is no wonder that he has been a friend of Martin Luther King, Jr. and an admirer of Nelson Mandela. It is no surprise that feminists see him as a friend and that, when his own Southern Baptist Convention stands opposed to the ordination of women, James' voice can be heard in response, shouting, "NO!"

James Dunn articulates a kingdom theology for a kingdom he wants to see actualized on earth, even as it exists in heaven. He believes Christians ought to work for transformation of the social order so that the values of God's kingdom might be realized in political, economic, and familial structures. While not an idealist who believes the human race can create a Utopia without God, James nevertheless believes God has called us to change this world into the kind of world it ought to be. In so doing, we initiate the good work that will be complete at the coming of the Lord.

The political agenda of the Christian Coalition is often focused on family values. Although the Christian Coalition frequently irritates James, he shares many of their concerns. But the Christian Coalition disagrees with how James seeks to accomplish agreed-upon goals. James wants America to have strong families. That is why he is committed to seeing the minimum wage raised. After all, can there be a strong family when a parent does not have an income that will provide for children? He stands for a national health plan because he feels all families should have protection against catastrophic illnesses. He argues in favor of day care because the new welfare bill requires single parents to go to work, even when there is no adequate means of care for their children.

This man has made a lot of enemies in his day. But even his enemies respect his forthrightness, honesty, and commitment to what he believes is right. James Dunn does not look for applause, except for the applause that comes from nail-pierced hands.

(From left) Larry Chesser (BJC Director of Communications), James Dunn, and Tony Campolo at the BJC 60th Anniversary Celebration, Calvary Baptist Church, Washington DC, October 1996

A Texas-Bred,
Spirit - Led Baptist

—————— *John Newport* ——————

*I'm a Texas-bred, Spirit-led, Bible-teaching, revival-preaching,
recovering Southern Baptist. That's neither a boast nor a whimper,
just an explanation of "where I'm coming from," as the kids say.*
—*James Dunn*[1]

TO UNDERSTAND JAMES DUNN (b. 1932), the Baptist leader in
Washington, D.C., you need to know about the influences coming
from his early life in Texas. We can group these influences under
the rubrics of family, academia, churches and pastorates, Baptist
Student Union directorship and adjunct teaching, Christian Life
Commission directorship and denominational life, and personal
qualities. In the words that follow, you will read reflections on
Dunn's life gleaned from his article "Why I Am a Baptist" and his
doctoral dissertation, and from correspondence with Dunn
himself, Phil Cates, and Bill Webb.[2]

Family

My father and mother, William Thomas Dunn and Edith
Campbell Dunn, migrated to Fort Worth for Dad to go to
Brantley-Draughon Business School in 1925. He took out the
first milk truck for Vandervoort Dairies. Since he was a milkman, from the time I was 9 years old until I was 16, I helped him
on milk trucks, summers and Saturdays. Living on the east side

of Fort Worth and working on milk trucks for my dad and uncle allowed me to see and be a part of a slice of life in the African-American section of town and the Hispanic cafes and grocery stores that many Fort Worth white kids never experienced.

Practical Christianity was largely handed down to me by very practical parents. I grew up believing that it didn't matter much what you said unless it matched up with what you did. Applied Christianity was a term that resonated with me. So, eventually I majored in ethics in my Ph.D. work.

Mother and Daddy had no patience with pretension. They could not stand people "putting on." The other side of that coin of tough truthfulness, lived as well as said, was immense respect for every last person with whom they came in contact. They "loved folks just because they are folks," as T. B. Maston used to say.

My parents came by these virtues honestly. They took Scripture seriously. Boy, did they! Spiritual formation suffused every ordinary chore. Hymn singing accompanied daily duties.

When I was 8 and Marilyn McNeely was 6, we were both in the primary department at Evans Avenue Baptist Church. Her father, Dr. Edwin McNeely, was the minister of music, her mother, the pianist.

Marilyn and I got married on December 19, 1958. We had postponed our wedding date a couple of times because she kept insisting on being in car wrecks.

Academic Life

Public Schools

Marilyn and I had wonderful experiences in the Fort Worth public schools. We played in the same 80-member symphony orchestra in our high school that performed standard symphonic literature. I had 3 years of Spanish and learned more about it in high school than anyone taught in most colleges. I was able to effectively sleep through freshman English in college because I had studied with Bob Wood Edmondson in high school. Hey! How can you beat that for public school education?

College

I shifted from TCU [Texas Christian University] to Texas
Wesleyan [TWC] for several reasons, mostly economic and con-
venience. I could walk to TWC, and it cost less. I did continue to
see Marilyn while she was at Baylor. In fact, once I had a car, we
had several dates on the Baylor campus in Waco and down to
Salado to the Old Stagecoach Inn.

I had a heavy dose of Methodism at Texas Wesleyan College.
It was the right school for me: small enough to know everyone,
caring professors, a healthy atmosphere of experienced religion.

Dr. Walter Glick was my major professor when I shifted
from a music major to a history major. He was Billy Leonard's
[Baptist historian] major professor a little later, too. Glick was
incredibly important to my spiritual life as well as my academic
life. He was one of two or three who would join us at morning
watch, very early in the day, before we even went to 8 AM classes.
He was a devout lay preacher and missionary-minded Methodist
and a scholarly man who had gotten his Ph.D. at the University
of Texas with Prescott Webb, who was one of Frederic Jackson
Turner's disciples. He taught in Mexico for a spell under a
UNESCO program and had a warm personal relationship with
those of us in his always small classes.

Seminary

It was almost foregone that James would enroll in Southwestern
Seminary in Fort Worth. His educational experience at South-
western, which began in 1953, was drawn out over 13 years. While
James was still in his Bachelor of Divinity program, James Leo
Garrett, professor of theology, recognized Dunn's ability and urged
him to consider advanced research.

The paper I wrote for James Leo Garrett, that provoked his com-
ment that I should pursue a doctorate, was about the influence
of Wesleyan hymnody on Baptist theology. I became convinced
that singing the hymns of John and Charles Wesley probably had

more to do with modifying the hyper-Calvinism of early Baptists than all the theological tirades of preachers in Great Britain and colonial America. I still think so.

Upon completion of the B.D., Dunn entered the doctoral program under the direction of T. B. Maston, who had greatly influenced Dunn during his BSU days at Texas Wesleyan. Maston was a master teacher. Early in life he discovered his gift of teaching and cultivated it. His impact is seen in more than the vast numbers of students he influenced. He did not accept unquestioningly the traditional approaches to the study of ethics. It was not for him simply moral philosophy or practical theology or Christian sociology or any of the other routine understandings of the field of study. Rather, Maston fashioned a practical, philosophical, political, biblical, theological approach to the study of Christian ethics.

In addition to his organization of the subject, the content of his ethics courses defied neat categories. His ethic was not liberal, though his passion for justice often plunged him into league with liberal Christian ethicists. He could not be considered "fundamentalist" as fundamentalists are usually perceived, but he took the Bible seriously. His teaching could not be honestly labeled neoorthodox, even though many of the insights of neoorthodoxy informed his perspective.[3]

Maston was widely known for beginning with the ethical teachings of the Bible as he dealt with any ethical issue or moral problem. While others might look to some other source of authority to give direction and form the ethical underpinnings, Maston was unapologetic in insisting that the basic ethical principles should be derived from the Bible. That biblical basis should be correctly interpreted and applied to daily life. According to Maston, the Bible teaches that ethical living finds its beginning in a dynamic religious experience and that a person's moral conduct is the fruit of a warm personal relationship with God. A deepening relationship with God keeps humans morally accountable and alert to the opportunities to serve God through service to others.[4]

Maston's emphasis upon practical religion appealed to Dunn, but probably more impressive than his lectures and writings to Dunn was his teacher's demonstration of a life lived in the significant commitment to the idea that everyone is made in the image of God.

A turning point in Dunn's interests and subsequent career was his research on the life and writings of J. M. Dawson, whose ministry was characterized by a passion for social justice, religious liberty, and Christian morality.

> I aspired at first to write on an ethic for juvenile justice because I'd been involved as a pastor in challenging the failures of the juvenile justice system in Texas. Then, when I went to West Texas State and was teaching credit Bible courses and dealt with the ideas of church-state separation, I decided we needed a Christian ethics dissertation on that tension. But when I got a letter from Dr. Robert A. Baker saying this is your second and final extension, I realized I had to write on a subject with an identifiable body of information. Jimmy Allen suggested J. M. Dawson.
>
> I had many visits with Dr. Dawson. Once I spent an entire day with him at the Navarro Hotel in Corsicana. During research I learned that he had written for publication from his first unsolicited story which was published in *the Dallas Morning News* when he was 14 until his death 80 years later.
>
> Dr. Dawson spoke to the Southern Baptist Convention in 1919 when it met in Atlanta, Georgia, on our responsibility to the Negro. In 1926, at the Southern Baptist Convention in Memphis, he preached on the plight of the sharecropper. He always had pacifistic tendencies and got in trouble with the Baylor board and other Baptist leaders for speaking out for peace in World War I and World War II.
>
> I do not believe members of the search committee of the Baptist Joint Committee even knew I'd written my doctoral dissertation on J. M. Dawson 14 years before when I got a call from Harold Bennett to ask if I would consider coming to lead the

Baptist Joint Committee. If there was any connection between my doctoral studies and my selection as executive director of the BJC, I never heard anyone mention it or refer to it.

The modest Joseph Martin Dawson in 1964 could hardly believe that his writings were to be the basis for a doctoral dissertation. He insisted that his chief contribution in the field of Christian ethics had been "where I took a stand, and things I have done, more than things I have written."

In the fifty years of Southern Baptist history, before J. M. Dawson penned his first article, Baptists in the South were too busy moving westward with the frontier, too consumed with pressing missionary claims, too devoted to the development of an organizational life consistent with Baptist peculiarities, to have time to write of the applications of the gospel to social problems.

The life of Joseph M. Dawson, spanning three-fourths of the history of Southern Baptists, says much about the social awakening of these people and their understanding of the meaning of religion for everyday life. Since he was consistently on the front edge of the denomination's ethical thought, an examination of Dawson's life may in some way measure the growth of ethical awareness among Southern Baptists and reveal the degree to which he shaped this concern.

After $31^1/_2$ years as the pastor of the First Baptist Church of Waco, after his 67th birthday, J. M. Dawson embarked upon a new career at the Baptist Joint Committee.

Robert G. Torbet, the American Baptist church historian, labeled Dawson a "modern Roger Williams" for his "statesmanlike defense of religious liberty." Torbet also recognized Dawson's role as the prime mover in the organization of POAU, Protestants and Other Americans United for the Separation of Church and State. He referred to Dawson as "the godfather" of POAU.

A perennial student, Dunn later did postdoctoral work at the London School of Economics and Political Science and engaged in extensive writing.

Churches and Pastorates

The dominant church for the Dunn family was Evans Avenue Baptist Church in Fort Worth. The pastor, Dr. Phelps, a Th.D. graduate in ethics under T. B. Maston, had considerable influence on James. Under Phelps' guidance, he began to glimpse the social aspects of the faith. Dunn was confronted with the discrepancy between his Christian faith and racial attitudes by a visiting speaker at Evans Avenue, Ralph Phelps, Jr., no relation to the pastor but another of Maston's Th.D. graduates. Dunn became angry and argued publicly with Phelps. For the next two or three years Dunn struggled with the racial issue, finally resolving it by his freshman or sophomore year in college.

> Evans Avenue was largely a people's church. The closest way we came to having professional people in the church were a large number of public school teachers and a couple of pharmacists.
>
> The pastors at Evans Avenue who influenced me were Dr. Loyed R. Simmons and Dr. Woodrow Wilson Phelps. I surrendered to the ministry at 19 in March of 1952, as Dr. W.W. Phelps said when I came down the aisle to make a commitment. As the choir sang "Wherever He Leads I'll Go," Phelps told the congregation: "Ah, James Dunn comes surrendering to preach." I asked him to please promptly and publicly correct that. The last thing I thought I would do is preach. Phelps then told the church: "I'm sorry; James is coming to surrender to the ministry, wherever that may lead."
>
> I started singing in Dr. McNeely's adult choir at Evans Avenue Church when I was 14, but I'd played the clarinet from the time I was 13 to 16. That's how I got to know the McNeelys. In fact, Marilyn's father was a far more dominant influence in my life than her mother or Marilyn during my first 10 years of

relationship to that family. Yes, Mac was the interim minister of music at Evans Avenue, and he remained interim minister of music for 25 years since Southwestern Baptist Theological Seminary would not allow faculty members to have full-time church jobs. He always dealt with seminary trade rules and regulations with his own flexible ethic.

Dunn began his professional ministerial service in 1954, serving as associate pastor at a church in Celina, Texas, for a year and at First Baptist Church in Weatherford, Texas, from 1955 to 1958, and then as pastor of Emmanuel Baptist Church from 1958 to 1961. While living in Weatherford, Dunn began a lifelong friendship with Jim Wright, a Presbyterian lay preacher who later became the Speaker of the U.S. House of Representatives.

> My years as a pastor, BSU director, evangelist, and mission volunteer have deeply imprinted my life with a commitment to experiential Christianity in which the opportunity and necessity of personal religion, volunteer commitment to Christ, and immediate access to God through Jesus Christ sum up my faith. I really came to internalize and intellectualize my basic belief when I faced what appeared to be for a time a terminal bout with cancer.
>
> In 1974 invasive melanoma planted me in the Stehlin Research Institute for a month and had me planning my funeral. I put aside theoretical argument, philosophical speculation, and any eschatological theories when I realized that they weren't worth much anyway. My faith was tested. I came to know "the peace that passes understanding."

Baptist Student Union Directorship
Adjunct Teaching

W. F. Howard, former director of student work for the Baptist General Convention of Texas, commented on Dunn's enthusiasm, vigor, and energy as BSU director at West Texas State University in

Canyon, Texas. Dunn was not only competent in his position, but he also became a great friend of the statewide student work and of W. F. Howard in particular.

> There was not a lazy bone in Dunn's body. He was like a push-all buzz saw who always kept going. He produced the goods. He had what it took to do the job in the Panhandle university. He greatly influenced the students. In his work as student director he never let me down as the state BSU director. He never disappointed me. He loved the Lord, he loved his work, and he loved students.

Dr. Howard noted that Dunn's personality was such that he sometimes made inappropriate comments. Dr. Howard mentioned that one of the fortunate things in Dunn's life was his marriage to Marilyn McNeely. "She would put her hand on his shoulder and calm this ball of energy down and balance out some of his statements."

Perhaps the best understanding of James Dunn as a BSU director came from Phil Cates, one of his students at West Texas State University. Cates later became a powerful member of the Texas legislature. Cates related personal incidents that furnish a remarkable insight into the work of James Dunn. According to Cates, James took the BSU to levels above those reached at the University of Texas or Baylor.

> James was thoroughly Texan. He told me he once received a Stetson hat from Amon Carter, the dramatic Texas publisher, himself. He defined being a Baptist Christian. He was loyal. He became a life coach for me.
>
> Having just passed my 51st birthday, almost 34 years after having met James Dunn, I recall that his capacity to passionately embrace change was the great lesson of our early relationship. This dynamic person took time to explain to a poor freshman concepts I had not heard of. But I distinctly remember his pointedly telling me that Bonhoeffer's thoughts on situation

ethics were not for me to ponder. It would only confuse me. I have the feeling that he had some rough struggles with these same concepts. Whatever James told me was without a doubt for my well-being. I instinctively knew this. He knew I knew. I didn't accept all that he said, but I did not offer infrequent refusal of his counsel with fear and trembling.

James was at once conservative, liberal, progressive, and a fundamentalist. The rightness of God's calling for this one man was intensely and passionately a daily war against Satan.

Our mid-winter retreat my freshman year was to Washington, D.C. We met with the doorkeeper of the House, Fishbait Miller, and Kentucky Republican Congressman John Sherman Cooper. We were privy to special treatment at the White House and the Soviet embassy. We toured the National Cathedral and Arlington National Cemetery. In past years the trip had been to Mexico City and other sites most Panhandle kids only read about. James offered a debt of richness unknown in the Panhandle and I've found rare in the world. He was always sensitive about any student's needing money for these events. Every time Dunn would ask if I could get the funds and offer to help if there were problems. I never needed help, but I know many students participated because Dunn dug in his own pocket and the pockets of other community leaders so people could participate without struggle.

These trips were only the tip of the work of James Dunn. Each day in Bible classes, vesper services, Friday night missions in Hereford and Amarillo, and counseling with members of the community, James made our lives rich beyond any reasonable degree.

Bill Webb, James' successor at West Texas State, affirmed that Dunn's years in Canyon were "formative and strengthening times" for the BSU, with the expansion of programs and missions and increased respect from the university and the community.

Texas Christian Life Directorship
Denominational Life

In November 1950, when Texas Baptists assembled in Fort Worth, T. B. Maston's committee, which had held three long meetings during the year, recommended the establishment of an agency designed to focus denominational attention on social concerns. The recommendation called for "an effective working combination of a conservative theology, and aggressive, constructive evangelism and a progressive application of the spirit and teachings of Jesus to every area of life." The Christian Life Commission of Texas was to be the vehicle through which these worthy objectives would be implemented.[5] James Dunn later became associate director and then director of the new ethics agency.

> Jimmy Allen tried to get me to be his associate in 1963 or 1964 but I was not through being a Bible instructor and BSU director. After Weston Ware left to become a BSU director in Hawaii, Jimmy came back to me in 1966 promising that he only wanted me for 2 to 3 years of service as an associate. I reluctantly agreed to that short-term assignment.
>
> I have no idea of how to begin to list key experiences of 14 years with the Texas CLC. We always were consumed with fighting liquor and gambling. We helped draw up and pass important legislation on drug abuse, juvenile justice, prison reform, workers' comp for farm workers, adequate pay for legislators, and a couple of dozen other specific legislative matters. We also worked to transform the emphasis on family life into a practical program that included marriage enrichment, family life education and leadership enablement for pastors and lay leaders in local churches. To this end, we brought on board Drs. David and Vera Mace. As far as I know, they were the only Quakers working for the BGCT.

The race relations challenge was always implicit in all of our attempts to apply Christianity. The rapidly shifting demography in Texas called me to spruce up my Spanish, and so I spent my first sabbatical, taken in Mexico City, in intensive Spanish study.

Since the 1960s the Christian Life Commission had often suggested legislative remedies to social injustices. This does not mean that the CLC had strayed from its Baptist roots. Indeed the agency has consistently striven for balance between evangelism and social activism. In 1967 the CLC stated its position concisely. It was equally "disturbed by the tendency . . . of some advocates of . . . social action to shrug off evangelism as if it were of secondary importance" and "by the attitudes of some evangelistically-minded men who treat the ethical demands of the gospel as handicaps to making converts." In fact, the Commission made a public statement affirming that "personal redemption and Christian social action belong together," for the Christian ethic is indissolubly joined with Christian conversion.[6]

If Jimmy Allen initiated the formal involvement of the CLC in politics, Dunn and his associate, Phil Strickland, broadened and refined the process. Together they involved the CLC more deeply in the political process than Allen had ever attempted. Because the CLC staff researched a wide range of public concerns, the Commission began regularly to offer informed testimony before state legislative committees. Soon, many legislators began to seek out the CLC as a knowledgeable source on public issues.[7]

At the same time that Dunn and Strickland expanded the lobbying activities of the CLC, they also sought to educate and inform fellow Baptists on political matters. To allay criticism of such political activism, Dunn never presumed to be the official spokesman of locally autonomous Baptist congregations. Despite the circumspection of Dunn and Strickland, the Commission's political activism still aroused the ire of many Baptists. Indeed, Dunn believed political activism was the most controversial aspect of his tenure.[8]

One of Dunn's lobbying efforts was in the Texas legislature on behalf of the Baptist General Convention of Texas. Phil Cates illustrates Dunn's political work:

> I had been elected for the state legislature by two votes with James' advice and direction. My office was, of course, his head-quarters. He never, never, never abused this use. During my first term Dunn yelled at Representative William S. "Bill" Heatley, chairman of the House Appropriation Committee, over some issue. James couldn't take pomposity from anyone. At that time only 2 or 3 members of the Texas House and Senate had all the power of state government through the purse strings. Mr. Heatley was at the top. He had given me $100 cash in my first campaign. I feared this confrontation between the two of them. I understood both. Representative Heatley could handle Baptist preacher types with ease until he came across James. In my opinion, what James took for pomposity was Heatley's way of brushing off preachers who often make a menace of themselves without understanding the weight of political power on a person. James would not be dismissed lightly. What Mr. Heatley took for another lilly-livered, milk-toast, words-only, pompous, typical, Baptist preacher was Dunn's effort to do right on a big level in the Texas political arena.

It is not surprising that Dunn's church-state address at New Orleans Baptist Seminary was titled "Called To Be Perpetually Indignant Prophets." Repeatedly, the CLC had implored Baptists to resist the allure of direct federal aid and to work for the separation of church and state.

Dunn received the Abner McCall Religious Liberty Award at Baylor in 1998. At the banquet for the awards presentation, Ray Burchett, Baylor alumni director, told Cates that he thought Dunn might finally cease railing against Baylor for supporting tuition equalization grants from the legislature to assist poor students attaining college degrees.

Beneath the surface Dunn was a theological conservative like T. B. Maston, who believed in the flawed nature of humanity and the tenacity of sin. This view influenced Dunn's approach to social problems. Though recognizing the necessity of social change, he pursued it cautiously. Dunn, in words strikingly reminiscent of Maston, said it plainly: "I'm an incrementalist, a reformer rather than a radical. I don't want to destroy institutions, but to improve them."[9]

Personal Qualities

Just as Dunn approaches reform in an incremental fashion, he deals with people in an accepting, unconditional manner. Of this Phil Cates comments:

> Dunn had no trouble handling the situation when he walked in on me while I was cleaning his office to see me drop some plaster Praying Hands that shattered on his office floor. Immediately he knew I was devastated. He told me that it was OK; they were only plaster. A park ranger whom Dunn had helped with drug recovery had made the Plaster Hands for James as a part of therapy, and sure they were significant, but without saying so much directly, James made me feel that I was more important than the shattered pieces of plaster. This, to me, was as close to God's love as I had ever felt.
>
> For me, James Dunn was with me, but maintained professional and classic detachment. Any man lucky and smart enough to marry the angel—Marilyn, equally talented and beautiful, and gracious—was a force to be considered as someone to pattern your life after.
>
> For me, to know James Dunn was the essence of unconditional love from the start.
>
> James Dunn has told me that I help him. I don't know how to handle this, but I accept it. He called when his daddy was ill and dying. He called when his mother was ill and dying. Today I

face these same life processes knowing of Dunn's faith in Jesus and of his spark for life in God's will that never dimmed.

On my having been selected as a distinguished alumnus at West Texas A&M, James sent me a framed copy of Scripture from Proverbs that says, "The poorest of all men is not the man without a cent, but the man without a dream." For me to work out my own dream was probably not possible without James Dunn. All of this from only a brief time of my life. All of this richly benefiting all the rest of my journey. God bless James Dunn.

Conclusion

Through the words of James Dunn and his associates and friends, this chapter has portrayed how Texas influences have helped to form one of America's unique and effective Christian leaders. Dunn's providentially developed career should also provide us with guidelines and encouragement for the challenges ahead.

Notes

[1]James Dunn, "Being Baptist," Everett C. Goodwin, ed. *Baptists in the Balance* (Valley Forge PA: Judson Press, 1997) 219.

[2]Used by permission.

[3]William M. Pinson, Jr., compiler/contributor, *An Approach to Christian Ethics* (Nashville: Broadman Press, 1979) 91, 92.

[4]Ibid.

[5]John W. Storey, *Texas Baptist Leadership and Social Christianity, 1900–1980* (College Station TX: A&M University Press, 1986) 168.

[6]Ibid., 223.

[7]Ibid., 169.

[8]Ibid., 170-71.

[9]Ibid., 148.

James Dunn (on right), Paschal High School Band,
Fort Worth TX, 1949

A Texan Goes to Washington
———— *Michael Smith* ————

AT FIRST BLUSH, any tenderhearted soul would feel for James Dunn and the agency he has run since January 1981, the Baptist Joint Committee on Public Affairs. It has been a rough eighteen-year tenure as head of the agency dedicated solely to religious liberty and the separation of church and state. The native Texan and Marilyn, his wife of almost fifty years, moved to Washington from Dallas just weeks prior to the inauguration of President Ronald Reagan, one of church-state separation's greatest foes. Five presidential elections have passed since James was named executive director of the BJC. Despite great odds, he and his scrappy agency still stand on Thomas Jefferson's wall of church-state separation, defending this traditional Baptist value against all who would knock it down.

James admits that January 1981 was a nervous time for church-state separation and for him personally. "Seeing Mr. Carter pack his bags and head back to Georgia as Marilyn and I were unpacking ours here in Washington was not a comforting sight. Losing Mr. Carter caused me to whimper about him not being here anymore. He was my friend and a strong supporter of church-state separation." James recalls being set straight early in his new job by Fred Wertheimer, then the president of Common Cause, which advocates campaign finance reform. "Oh, quit whining, Dunn,"

Wertheimer said, according to Dunn's recollection. "You've never been more needed."

In reflecting upon his tenure at the BJC, Dunn says that despite the hard knocks along the way, it has been a good experience for him personally. "The time in Washington and the job have been a unique pulpit from which to enunciate the distinctive Baptist take on the world of politics and religion," he said.

Before going to Washington as head of the BJC, James served for thirteen years as executive director of the Christian Life Commission, the ethics agency of the Baptist General Convention of Texas. It was from this position that Dunn ran the opposition campaigns on three separate statewide initiatives regarding parimutuel gambling, winning all three elections. The ethics agency was profiled in an August 26, 1973, article from the *New York Times*, where PBS journalist Bill Moyers commented on his longtime friend. Moyers is quoted as saying he had overheard an oil executive in Austin remark, "I'd rather have been Jacob wrestling with the angel than to see James Dunn walk in the door of my office." While in Texas, he served on the governor's Juvenile Justice Council, which helped to reform the state's juvenile justice system. Since moving to Washington, James has joined the boards of Americans United for Separation of Church and State and the Churches' Center for Theology and Public Policy. In 1985, he served as president of Bread for the World, a faith-based organization that ministers to the needs of the hungry and malnourished.

"He is the conscience of millions of Baptists, which is an awesome and heavy responsibility," said W. Christian Sizemore, president of William Jewell College in Liberty, Missouri. "But (it's) a task from which James Dunn has never flinched." Sizemore's college, the only college in America aligned with both the American Baptist Churches, U.S.A., and a Southern Baptist state convention, presented James with an honorary doctorate in 1996. While serving as president of Alderson Broaddus College in Phillipi, W. Va., Sizemore presented James his first honorary degree in 1990. "He has served us (Baptists) well," Sizemore said. Central Baptist Theological Seminary in Kansas City, Kansas, an American Baptist seminary that now receives support from the Cooperative Baptist Fellowship, presented Dunn with its Distinguished Service Award in 1991. And Baylor University in Waco, Texas, presented him with its Abner V. McCall Religious Liberty Award in 1998.

As executive director of the BJC, James spent about 100 days each year on the road spreading the good news of religious liberty. The Texan's eight frequent-flyer accounts, each with a separate airline company, are evidence of his commitment to the cause. He has racked up more than 500,000 miles on just one of his eight accounts. Dunn crisscrosses the country visiting churches, seminaries, universities, and colleges, reminding fellow Baptists about their traditional stand for religious liberty and church-state separation. "He's been on this campus to speak and teach on an average of once a year for many years," Sizemore said.

"The Rosa Parks of the religious liberty issue," is how U.S. Representative Chet Edwards (D-TX) describes Dunn. Edwards worked closely with the BJC in 1998 to defeat the Religious Freedom Amendment sponsored by Representative Ernest Istook (R-OK). Istook's bill would have amended the U.S. Constitution to allow state-sponsored prayer in public schools, religious displays on public property, and taxpayer funds to go to religious schools. "James Dunn was almost elected by the Lord for this position during this period of time," said Grady Cothen, head of the Sunday School Board of the SBC from 1974 to 1984. "James Dunn has shown enormous moral courage," Cothen added. "I would think it would have been very difficult for anyone to have done a better job." Dunn today refers to the years of SBC troubles lightly. "In baseball the American League has a designated hitter. For a decade I was the designated 'hittee' of Southern Baptist fundamentalists," he said.

"James Dunn has been exceedingly effective despite being exceedingly embattled," said Jimmy Allen, pastor of the Chapel at

Big Canoe, Georgia, and president of the Southern Baptist Convention (SBC) from 1977 to 1979. Dunn has "never wavered on the cause of freedom of conscience," he added. Foy Valentine, executive director of the Christian Life Commission of the SBC from 1960 to 1988, said that Dunn has been "courageous, insightful, energetic, and significantly effective." Valentine also pointed out that his friend has been very outspoken. "He's not prone to pussyfooting and to softening his stand," he said. Leading the BJC has been Dunn's "special calling," traveling "along in the path that J. M. Dawson began to clear," Valentine said.

Some might say that it is providential that Dunn heads the agency founded and led by J. M. Dawson, the great defender of church-state separation. While at seminary, Dunn wrote his doctoral dissertation on the "Ethical Thought of Joseph Martin Dawson." Fifteen years after he wrote about the BJC's first executive director, Dunn was asked to take the helm of the agency. "I had no idea when I wrote my doctoral dissertation on Dawson that I would ever someday sit in his chair," he said. Dunn credits T. B. Maston, longtime chair of the Christian Ethics Department at Southwestern Seminary, as another great influence. "He was my mentor," Dunn said of Maston, who taught at the seminary for forty years. "I don't mind being considered a disciple of T. B. Maston, though it's a daunting challenge," he said. "Through all the racial wars of the 1950s and 1960s, Maston was the courageous pioneer of Christian ethics in Southern Baptist life," Dunn said. "He was the father of the Baptist emphasis on Christian ethics and the mentor of literally dozens of ministers, missionaries, and professors," he added. "Other than my parents, Dawson and Maston were the most formative figures in my Christian life."

"In an age of nuclear giants and moral midgets, James Dunn stands like a redwood tree," Oliver Thomas, special counsel for civil and religious liberties for the National Council of Churches of Christ and former general counsel for the BJC, said of his friend and former boss. Albert Pennybacker of the National Council of

Churches called Dunn "the most effective advocate for a genuinely religious understanding of public issues of any church representative in Washington." Pennybaker said that Dunn is an advocate, not a lobbyist. "An advocate serves the interest of the common good. It's a ministry to him," he said.

One would be hard-pressed to overdramatize the trials and tribulations the BJC faced in the past two decades. The mere fact that the small, Washington, D.C.-based agency is still up and running is no small feat. "About like David and Goliath," is how Jimmy Allen describes the BJC in its battles in defense of religious liberty and the separation of church and state. The agency has weathered years of attacks from fundamentalist leaders within the SBC, who eventually cut off all funding to the agency. Despite these assaults on the agency and the principles it defends, the BJC and its allies have successfully shielded the bedrock Baptist principle of religious liberty and church-state separation from powerful secular and religious forces determined to send them both to the dustbin of history. Despite these odds, not only has the BJC survived, it also thrives, as does Thomas Jefferson's wall separating church and state.

"The (BJC) has fulfilled an absolutely unbroken string of principled presence in support of religious liberty and the separation of church and state," said Foy Valentine. "You don't maintain religious liberty without the separation of church and state," he said. The agency "has maintained a principled commitment to the separation of church and state as a guarantee of religious liberty" throughout its more than half-century history.

Throughout American history many individuals and organizations have existed that failed to value soul freedom and true religious liberty. And ever since the colonies were formed, Baptists have been on the scene to advocate for the need for a church and a state that are totally independent from one another.

The past two decades have been a particularly contentious period in regard to church-state issues. "Church-state separation and religious liberty are (facing) their greatest hazard that they've faced in generations," said Grady Cothen. During the 1980s and 1990s the principal of separation of church and state has faced a confederacy of well-organized and well-financed foes like it has never seen before in the history of the Republic. "There have been many assaults on the wall of separation of church and state and the First Amendment during my time here," Dunn said. The Reagan administration, and to a lesser degree the Bush administration, was hostile to church-state separation, and pushed legislation and appointed judges to the federal courts who shared their hostility. The U.S. Congress has at various times abandoned historic respect for church-state separation.

The fundamentalist takeover of the SBC led the denomination to jettison the convention's historic and well-documented stand for separation. Religious Right organizations such as the Christian Coalition gained great influence in the Republican Party. Fundamentalist leaders such as Jerry Falwell, Pat Robertson, and James Dobson made it a priority of their ministries to call for separation's demolition. And the U.S. Catholic bishops, traditionally no friend of church-state separation, continued to demand that tax monies go to support parochial schools. "We're in for a long-haul battle (over church-state issues) with the forces who are allied with the right-wing element in this country," said Jimmy Allen, the last theologically moderate president of the SBC.

Foy Valentine, who resides in Dallas where he edits the journal *Christian Ethics Today*, believes that despite the best effort of some to dismantle the First Amendment, religious liberty will survive. He credits the "deep wisdom of the founding thinkers, shakers, and movers of this nation" for devising the First Amendment. These liberties "will not be permanently crushed by greedy and grasping partisans who seek public money for private purposes," Valentine said. "The law of the land may be bent a little bit, but in the long run, this incredibly beautiful principle of church-state separation is destined to survive and to thrive." Valentine said he believes "history is not on the side of despots and seekers of special privilege. But it is on the side of freedom and truth embodied in what the (BJC) has stood for."

While helping to successfully defend religious liberty from assault, the BJC has had to fight for its own survival. Upon winning the SBC presidency in 1979, the fundamentalist leadership began to attack Dunn personally as well as the BJC as a whole. In a systematic campaign of intimidation, harassment, and firings lasting over a decade, the fundamentalist leaders were able to purge all the heads of SBC agencies and seminaries. These lifelong denominational workers were quickly replaced with men who agreed with the fundamentalists' views on Scripture and politics. Allen believes the fundamentalists have no comprehension of true religious liberty. "They believe more in power than in freedom," Allen said. "If you want government money for your programs, you can't believe in the separation of church and state," he added. Ironically, the one agency head the fundamentalists were unable to bag was their first and most coveted target, James Dunn. Paige Patterson, current SBC president and one of the key architects of the fundamentalist takeover, was an early and constant critic of Dunn and the BJC. In 1982 Patterson said of Dunn, "I think there will be something done to silence him."

Grady Cothen said the fundamentalists put a high priority on removing Dunn and on weakening the agency. The fundamentalists said, "Let's get James Dunn out of the way so we can do as we please," according to Cothen. Valentine agrees. "Dunn was seen as a barrier to the effort to get parochiaid for their private institutes for their own aggrandizement. They wanted government support and tax money, and Dunn stood in the way," Valentine said.

Dunn was able to survive because the BJC receives support from numerous separate Baptist denominations, not just the SBC, which controlled only about one-third of the forty-five-member policymaking board. Many Baptist conventions and conferences in the United States support the BJC: American Baptist Churches in the U.S.A.; Baptist General Conference; National Baptist Convention of America; National Baptist Convention, USA, Inc.; National Missionary Baptist Convention; North American Baptist Conference; Progressive National Baptist Convention, Inc.; Religious Liberty Council; Seventh-Day Baptist General Conference. The state Baptist conventions of North Carolina, Virginia, Kentucky, and Texas also directly support the BJC.

Even though Patterson and his allies failed to force Dunn out at the BJC and to take over the agency, they did succeed in cutting the agency out of the SBC budget. This process was accomplished in three steps culminating at the 1991 SBC meeting. Up until the "defunding," the SBC provided more than half of the BJC's financing. "When they were unable to get (rid of) Dunn, the (fundamentalists) substituted the Baptist Joint Committee with a Political Action Committee," Cothen said. The SBC's new entity, the Ethics and Religious Liberty Commission (ERLC), formerly the Christian Life Commission, no longer supports traditional Baptist views on church-state separation. The ERLC pushes for school-sponsored prayer and tax monies for parochial schools, along with other goals that are anathema to Baptist tradition since the times of Roger Williams and John Leland. The SBC leadership continues to navigate the denomination into partisan political waters. At their 1993 convention, Southern Baptists passed a resolution that condemned President Bill Clinton and Vice-President Al Gore, both lifelong Southern Baptists, for supporting abortion rights. Richard Land, president of the SBC's ERLC, has talked of the need for the Republican Party to become more responsive to the will of the Christian Right. "The go-along, get-along strategy is dead. No more engagement. We want a wedding ring, we want a ceremony, we want a consummation of the marriage," Land said as quoted in the March 23, 1998 edition of *The New York Times*.

"At the time it was like being disowned by my family," Dunn said about being cut off from the SBC. "But looking back on it, because of the affirmation we've received since then by authentic Baptists, it has been a blessing in disguise." In addition to national and state denominational bodies, almost 700 individual Southern Baptist congregations currently support the BJC with funding. With an annual budget of almost $880,000, the agency's largest financial contributor is the Cooperative Baptist Fellowship. The CBF, a grouping of moderate Southern Baptists, accounts for about thirty percent of the BJC's budget.

"Without question, Dunn's greatest feat was ensuring that the agency maintained its integrity while under fire from the (SBC)," wrote Pam Parry in her 1996 book, *On Guard for Religious Liberty*. According to Parry, "Under duress, the agency never wavered from the bedrock Baptist principal that separation of church and state is the best way to safeguard religious liberty. Adherence to this principle, in the face of intense pressure, was even more significant than the agency's survival."

Despite the trials of the past two decades, the BJC is as effective a defender of religious liberty as ever. The agency, the nation's only faith-based organization that deals exclusively with religious liberty and church-state separation issues, continues to stand its ground on issues such as school-sponsored prayer, tax monies to parochial schools, and the rights of religious minorities. It took the likes of a J. M. Dawson to found the Baptist Joint Committee and to guarantee that America has such a voice for soul freedom, religious liberty, and the separation of church and state. And it has taken the likes of a James Dunn to keep that witness alive and effective in such perilous and trying times.

Dunn's Election as Executive Director, BJC, October 1980

Mentor to a Senator
——— *Mark O. Hatfield* ———

HOW DOES ONE enumerate all of the contributions James Dunn has made to the cause of Christ and the advancement of the Kingdom? A many-faceted man with unique skills such as James Dunn leaves footprints in multiple areas of life—from rural to urban America, from the wastelands of Texas to the verdant forests of Oregon to the nation's capital. He has made numerous contributions to my life. Here I will focus on one of these.

James Dunn taught me in vivid terms about my Baptist heritage and tradition as he engaged in battles for religious liberty and the separation of church and state. He brought me writings and admonitions about remaining true to Baptist distinctives as we live our Christian witness, but always in a kindly, non-acerbic manner. With a clearer perspective of Christian church history through its many eras and of Baptist history from the seventeenth century to the twenty-first, I came to better understand current church-state issues.

Because of Dunn's influence, I reread the legacy of Constantine and his proclaiming Rome to be Christian in AD 312. Up to that point, the Christian community paid their taxes but refused to bow to the state and pagan gods. They considered such to be diametrically opposed to the commandments of Christ; Christ was their only Lord, and he prevented them from swearing an oath to the state. Likewise, they refused to serve on juries or in the army.

Because of these convictions, some church historians have claimed that at no other time has the Christian community been so unified.

Constantine's conversion was followed by a deal he made with early church leaders: (1) clergy were exempt from paying taxes and serving military duty; (2) the church was allowed to set up its own court system; and (3) church authorities were permitted to own and receive property. Constantine gained the support and, in time, the allegiance of this early church. A new infusion of "Christian" soldiers entered the military to protect a "Christian state" against a heathen world. No wonder Baptist history is rich with wise suspicion toward all "power," political and ecclesiastical alike.

I remember discussions with Dunn over our shared concern that some of our fellow Christians today embrace the Constantinian doctrine that a government made up of Christians can make a nation Christian. We were often amazed that Christians believed government might be able to legislate or command our relationship to Christ. We agreed that the lordship of Christ cannot be established in a state founded on pluralism and diversity. The lordship of Christ can be established only in the hearts of individual people.

William R. Estep's fine little book, *Revolution Within the Revolution*, which James gave me, reminded me of the important role we Baptists played in insisting upon complete religious freedom and the separation of church and state. Many colonists involved in the founding of the Massachusetts Bay Colony had escaped the state church of England to worship freely in the New World. But in time, conformity displaced freedom, and the colonial church became a tax-supported church. Dissidents such as Baptists, Jews, and Quakers were eventually driven out of the Puritan colony for non-conformance.

Among many justifications for this politicization of the church were the eloquent words of John Cotton in "A Discourse about Civil Government":

Theocracy, or to make the Lord our governor, is the best form of
government in a Christian commonwealth ... wherein the men
chosen by them are godly men and fitted with a spirit of government ... in which the laws they rule by are the laws of God.[1]

But early Baptist leader Roger Williams challenged the concept
of a church that can truly embrace all citizens of a given country:

We query where you now find one footstep, print, or pattern in
this doctrine of the Son of God for a national holy covenant and
so, consequently ... a national church? Where find you evidence
of a whole nation, country or kingdom converted to the faith,
and of Christ's appointing of a whole nation or kingdom to walk
in one way of religion? Again we ask whether ... the constitution
of a national church ... can possibly be framed without a rack-
ing and tormenting of souls as well as of the bodies of persons,
for it seems not possible to fit it to every conscience.[2]

History indeed bestows insight that comes from no other
source. It gives the opportunity to judge the experiment, to test and
validate the successes and failures of the past, and provides us the
ability to maximize successes and minimize repeated failures.

In modern times, tensions have grown around the church-state
issue relating to school prayer. In 1962 the Supreme Court ruled
mandated school prayer unconstitutional because it violated the
separation of church and state.[3] As with many other things in the
political world, there ensued an overreaction on all sides of the
issue. Some actually believed the high court had made it impossible for individual students to pray within the confines of a public
school—as if all prayer had to be audible and as if the Supreme
Court could rule out silent prayer. Lower courts overreacted by
ruling against student Bible study in public educational facilities.

In the *Widmar* case involving the University of Missouri at
Kansas City, the Supreme Court clarified the issue of religious
activity at state-supported colleges and universities by stating that

once an institution of higher learning established the "right to forum," it could not dictate the content of the forum. Thus, the Court in effect made the issue one of free speech instead of religious freedom.[4]

James Dunn again was quick to see the balance and fairness of this ruling and was deeply involved in legislation that Congressman Don Bonker (D-WA) and I co-sponsored known as the Equal Access Act. This bill sought to apply the teachings of Widmar to our nation's public secondary schools.

Under the provisions of this legislation, if a school allows even one noncurriculum-related group to meet, it must allow student-initiated religious groups to meet, too. In short, religious groups were to have "equal access" to school fora and facilities to hold club meetings. Faculty members can be present at the meetings, but may not sponsor or participate in them.

As James Dunn campaigned for equal access legislation, he was demonstrating that Christians and other religious groups should not be discriminated against or given special privileges. He asked only for fair treatment. He was instrumental in mobilizing people of many faiths, along with organizations concerned with civil liberties.

The Equal Access Act was passed on August 11, 1984, and on June 4, 1990, the Supreme Court upheld the constitutionality of the Act in the *Mergens* case.[5] This was a major milestone for both religious freedom and freedom of speech in public schools.

James Dunn also played a critical role in the introduction and passage of the Religious Freedom Restoration Act, whose purpose was to restore a high standard by which religious liberty claims were to be evaluated. Again, this was supported by most of the organizations covering the major religions. Unfortunately, in 1997 the Supreme Court overturned the Religious Freedom Restoration Act in part by declaring it unconstitutional as applied to state and local governments.[6]

Indeed, these were significant political and religious moments in our great nation. They perpetuate the dynamic tension of the First Amendment even to this day. No less a person than Alexis de Toqueville observed the American experience, commenting in the 1840s:

> As long as religion rests upon those sentiments which are the consolation of all affliction, it may attract the affections of mankind. But if it be mixed up with the bitter passions of the world, it may be constrained to defend allies whom its interests, and not the principle of love, have given to it; or to repel as antagonists men who are still attached to its own spirit, however opposed they may be to the powers to which it is allied. The Church cannot share the temporal power of the state without being the object of a portion of that animosity which the latter excites.[7]

The reader of this tribute to James Dunn may make his or her own application to any similarities with current issues and "Christian" political activities.

James Dunn is concerned about freedom of religion for everyone, for no one group can enjoy freedom unless all groups can practice their faith and unless even the nonbeliever's conscience is protected.

Baptists played important roles in the early days of the Reformation. Similarly, in our day James Dunn has given leadership to Baptists in safeguarding freedom of religion for every person and in preserving the freedom to practice our faith, to evangelize, and to persuade. He has also taught us how crucial the separation of church and state is to ensuring that government cannot legislate convictions.

Thank you, James, for being a great mentor. I wish you well in your retirement—but never retire from teaching.

Notes

[1]Quoted in William R. Estep, *Revolution within the Revolution* (Grand Rapids: Eerdmans, 1990) 74.

[2]Ibid., 75-76.

[3]*Engel v. Vitale,* 370 U.S. 421 (1962).

[4]*Widmar v. Vincent,* 454 U.S. 263 (1981).

[5]*Board of Education v. Mergens,* 496 U.S. 226 (1990).

[6]*City of Boerne v. Flores,* 117 S. Ct. 2157 (1997).

[7]Alexis de Toqueville, *Democracy in America,* vol. 1, ch. XVII, part iii (1840).

Senator Mark Hatfield and James Dunn confer during an editors' briefing in the senator's office in Washington, D.C., in 1986.

James Dunn—
A Fictional Character?

A. James Rudin

OF COURSE JAMES M. DUNN DOES NOT REALLY EXIST. The man we know and admire is, in fact, a brilliantly created invention of two famous novelists: Larry McMurtry and Mark Twain.

James is a McMurtry "good ole boy" character who possesses an unmistakable Texas twang that successfully accomplishes two goals: it reminds everyone of his native Texas origins, and it disarms folks, especially religious and political leaders, who are not prepared for James' astute mind and probing intellect. The Texas accent is a device that a gifted novelist like McMurtry would give to one of his central characters.

McMurtry's people always have what literary critics call "texture" and "depth." These terms mean that behind James' "Aw shucks! I'm just a good ole boy from Fort Worth" façade resides a man with a steel-trap mind and a spiritual core who understands precisely what is going on in American religious and political circles. And like a McMurtry character, James is fully engaged in life with all its complexities and nuances.

Read *The Adventures of Huckleberry Finn* and *The Adventures of Tom Sawyer* and you will find that Mark Twain, albeit a writer whose values were shaped during the last century, clearly had James Dunn in mind when he created those two immortal figures of American literature. Huck's friendship with Jim, the African American, and Tom's relationship with Injun Joe are examples of

people crossing the ugly barriers of bigotry and prejudice. Indeed, combating racism in all its forms has been a hallmark of James Dunn's public career. Mark Twain would have liked James because both of them share the gift for great storytelling and have insights into the human condition.

One of my first encounters with James Dunn was in 1977 when we worked together on an interreligious conference that took place at Southern Methodist University in Dallas. The conference theme was "Agenda for Tomorrow: Baptists and Jews Face the Future." The meeting focused on the often unacknowledged relationship between religion and the American political process. Several hundred laypersons, pastors, and rabbis attended the meeting, and there were sessions on human rights, world hunger, and, of course, religious liberty. It was a pioneering effort both for my organization, the American Jewish Committee (AJC), and for James' Christian Life Commission of the Baptist General Convention of Texas.

Some critics in the Jewish community were concerned that the AJC was too deeply involved with benighted and ultraconservative Southern "crackers" or "rednecks." And some elements within Southern Baptist life viewed any conference with Jews in only one light: as an opportunity to engage in conversion efforts. That Jews and Southern Baptists perceived each other in such harsh terms clearly revealed just how large was the abyss that separated our two communities of faith. It also revealed how much work needed to be done to overcome stereotypes and to strengthen religious pluralism.

Despite the angry snipers in both camps, we pressed ahead, and, of course, the conference was a great success in many ways. It was one of the first times that a national Jewish organization recognized the growing importance of Southern Baptists in the American political and cultural scene. It also marked an important milestone in the SBC's relationship with the Jewish community in the United States.

Because James Dunn was directly involved in a major way, that 1977 Dallas meeting revealed to the Jewish community that there were courageous Southern Baptist leaders who were prepared to take principled public stands on critical issues such as religious liberty, separation of church and state, and the duty of religious communities to make their voices heard within the public arena on issues of vital concern. It was a message the Jewish community needed to hear from an important segment of the American Christian community.

Three years later, in 1980, Bailey Smith, president of the Southern Baptist Convention, delivered an address in Dallas that received wide media coverage. In his speech Smith declared that "God Almighty does not hear the prayer of a Jew," and his words set off a firestorm of controversy and protest.

Of special interest was the fact that many Southern Baptists joined with other Christians in strongly repudiating Smith's statement. Among those who protested the SBC president's words was James Dunn. His secure grounding in his own faith provided him an excellent religious anchor. Because of this grounding in his own tradition, James, in 1980 and throughout his entire career, has been an articulate and compelling voice for religious pluralism.

James Dunn always reminds me that Southern Baptists are, by definition and disposition, "a bunch of stubborn, independent people." But it took courage to publicly criticize the president of his own denomination. He is always embarrassed when I call him a modern Roger Williams or John Leland, two of James' spiritual heroes. But he really is the living embodiment of those early Baptist champions of religious liberty and freedom of conscience.

I rejoiced when James assumed the professional leadership of the Baptist Joint Committee in Washington. With his Texas pedigree and his graduate school training in Great Britain, he was a natural for the job. James' deep friendship with many of our nation's political leaders is an important aspect of his work, but he never forgets that above all he is a pastor. That unique combination of political sophistication and genuine religious faith is a rare commodity in Washington. It is always in extremely short supply, and nothing in recent years has changed this sad fact.

Leaders are frequently judged not only by their friends, but also by the opponents they attract. Naturally, an outspoken champion of the First Amendment and a leader in the fight to maintain the historic constitutional principle of church-state separation will make enemies. James is no exception. Sadly, James has had myriad exhausting and bitter battles with a host of adversaries who either disagree sharply with his public stands or seek to undermine the strength and effectiveness of his beloved Baptist Joint Committee.

Happily, James and the BJC both survived the difficult years, and it soon became clear to me that the struggles had tempered James and made him an even stronger leader. For proof, listen to him anytime he speaks about the preciousness of personal religious liberty. Listen to him when he speaks about the meaning of the First Amendment. Listen to him attack the frequent pernicious attempts in Congress to mandate prayers and Bible reading in America's public schools. He is fiery, humorous, and always well-informed when he testifies before Congress or addresses a public gathering. Whenever I hear him speak, I am glad to be on his side of the barricade.

One of James' lasting achievements was his work in 1993 and 1994 on the document "A Shared Vision." Although James always speaks of it as a joint product of the BJC, the AJC, and the National Council of Churches, the truth is that James and his colleagues were the intellectual and spiritual driving force behind this significant statement.

"A Shared Vision" is James at his best. The document is a powerful and reasoned defense of our nation's long history of church-state separation and religious liberty. It asserts that no American should be made to feel an outcast because of religious beliefs or the lack of a faith commitment. Sentence after sentence describes the continuing American experiment in religious freedom.

"A Shared Vision" was released in 1994 in an elaborate ceremony where James formally presented the document to fellow
Southern Baptist, Vice-President Al Gore. In the years since, hun-
dreds of thousands of copies have been widely distributed in
churches, synagogues, schools, colleges, universities, seminaries,
and government institutions. Historians may someday see "A
Shared Vision" as one of the most important interreligious
statements of the 1990s.

Perhaps if "A Shared Vision" had simply made the case for
church-state separation and religious liberty, it would have been
adequate. But what makes the document unique is its acknowledg-
ment that religion and religious people have a legitimate role to
play in shaping American society, including its public schools.
James' influence is clearly at work in the sections of it that urge
religiously-motivated people to participate fully in the business of
deciding what kind of society we are and what kind of society we
will become.

This kind of complex, nuanced position is James' special
contribution to the issue. His fervent, passionate defense of the traditional position of church-state separation is matched by his
equally fervent, passionate demand that people of faith enter the
political system. I am always stirred and impressed by James'
supreme confidence in the ability of Americans to create a viable
religiously pluralistic democracy.

He believes that the tent of religious freedom is large enough
and its supports strong enough to house not only Jews and Christians, but also Americans of other faiths. James' staunch Texas
Southern Baptist belief system is wide enough and deep enough to
affirm the rights of Muslims, Hindus, Buddhists, Sikhs, and all
other religious groups in America. His religious faith is also strong
enough to affirm with the same vigor the rights of those Americans who do not profess a faith. James' vision of America demands
freedom of conscience for every citizen.

James and I participated in a dramatic session at the American Jewish Committee's 1995 Annual Meeting in Washington, when we were the official respondents to Ralph Reed. Reed was then the president of the Christian Coalition, and both he and his organization had attracted extensive media coverage. The Christian Coalition was seen by some people as an irresistible force in American politics, especially after the Republican Party's success in the 1994 congressional elections. Others, including James and myself, were concerned about the exclusivist character of the Christian Coalition and its announced agenda.

Many members of the Christian Coalition were Southern Baptists, and many Jews believed that this represented a retreat from traditional SBC positions regarding church-state separation and other critical domestic issues. Following Reed's presentation at the AJC meeting, James spoke eloquently about his own personal commitment to a progressive political agenda and to the strict separation of church and state.

James' clear remarks were warmly received; they provided the large audience with another perspective of the evangelical Christian community—one that differed significantly from Reed's views. Indeed, the two Christians, Dunn and Reed, vigorously debated several key policy questions at the AJC meeting, and their spiritual interchange attracted media attention. As a direct result of James' words, the American Jewish Committee members had a much clearer picture of both the Christian Coalition and the basic differences of opinion and policy that exist within the evangelical community. As usual, James was focused, insightful, and cogent in his response to Reed.

On other issues that impact directly upon the Jewish community, James has, as the saying goes, "always been there." Two examples will graphically illustrate this point.

James has been a stalwart friend of the State of Israel in good times and bad. He has consistently supported Israel in its long quest for security in a turbulent area of the globe. I have always been deeply appreciative of his support because during the five decades of Israel's independence, it has sometimes, alas, been fashionable in certain Christian circles to hold the Jewish State to a double standard of behavior. That is, Israel has often been judged by some Christian leaders with a different set of ethical weights and measures. The Bible, however, demands that we employ the same weights and measures in all cases of judgment, and this is something James has done *vis-a-vis* the Middle East throughout his long and distinguished career.

In the mid 1990s James and I were pulpit guests at a Sabbath service in Boca Raton, Florida. Nearly a thousand people were present that Friday evening at Temple Beth-El when James delivered the sermon. In his message James spoke with his usual fervor about the importance of maintaining the separation of church and state in America. But he was careful to note that his passionate insistence on separation was only a means of protecting religion from inroads and control by government. The First Amendment and America's two centuries of religious freedom had guaranteed that religion in the United States would be robust, spiritually exciting, and entirely voluntary.

As the sermon unfolded, James eschewed Christian attempts, whether open or covert, to convert Jews to Christianity. His own deep religious faith allows others to express theirs, and he is no less a Southern Baptist because he does not seek the conversion of the Jews. Of course, there are those in the SBC who take a totally different stance, but, as usual, James stood his theological ground even when the SBC in 1996 adopted a resolution calling for increased "evangelizing of the Jews."

Then there is the personal side of James Dunn. Many of his "buttoned-down" colleagues in both the Christian and Jewish communities are at first put off by his use of picturesque idioms and figures of speech to convey his thoughts. These folks are more accustomed to such phrases as "a misguided political leader with whom I differ," than to James' more direct and usually accurate, "That guy's a wily rascal."

As a result, sometimes people meeting James for the first time need a course in what I call "Dunnspeak." Its lexicon of phrases contains earthy descriptions of adversaries and opponents. But "Dunnspeak" also contains original expressions of respect and friendship. One example of "Dunnspeak" is most vivid in my mind.

Some years ago James and I were working together on a project. There was a deadline involved, and James, as is often the case, was on the road somewhere urging his fellow Americans to stand tall for the First Amendment and freedom of religion. I caught up with him by telephone, and he excitedly (is James ever not excited?) told me that everything was in order and he had completed his assigned task. James said, "Jim, you can put your head safely to the pillow tonight assured that the thing has been taken care of."

What a comforting and apt phrase that is! In the many years James has served as executive director of the Baptist Joint Committee, I and millions of other Americans have been able to put our heads to the pillow secure in the knowledge that the First Amendment has a passionate and effective champion in the nation's capital. We've put our heads to the pillow secure in the knowledge that the historic principle of church-state separation has a passionate and effective champion. Most of all, we have happily put our heads to the pillow secure in the knowledge that a gifted and creative leader like James Dunn is there in Washington battling for religious freedom every day.

James Dunn is, quite simply, an original. As a Jew, as a rabbi, and as an American, I am thankful that James is not a fictional character from the pages of a novel, but is instead a flesh-and-blood servant of the God who commands him and us to be free men and women.

In the Jewish tradition we salute such a person with the toast, "May you live, be well, and continue your vital work until you are 120." When he reaches that advanced age, we will then ask God to grant James Dunn more years so he can "do his extraordinary thing."

Rabbi A. James Rudin

James Dunn and Ralph Reed at the 1996 American Jewish Committee Annual Meeting, Washington DC

A Chihuahua Who Thinks He's a German Shepherd

Oliver S. Thomas

HUMANS ARE HERD ANIMALS. Read our history, and you'll discover that for centuries we traveled in small bands—tribes, if you will—hunting and gathering for our survival.

We're still herd animals. We may live in smaller, nuclear families, but we "group up" every chance we get: gangs, bridge clubs, service clubs, churches, political parties. If we are not lemmings, we are close to it. We go along to get along. There is enormous peer pressure among adults in the United States to avoid saying anything that might offend. The need to preserve peace and tranquility explains part of it, but mostly it's born of *fear*—our innate need to be accepted as part of the group and the fear that speaking out could lead to rejection.

There is a certain hypocrisy born of this tendency. A sort of playacting, as the literal meaning of "hypocrisy" suggests. Admittedly, a certain degree of duplicity is required in all human relations. To do otherwise would generate endless conflict and inflict unnecessary pain.

Imagine: "No, honey, I don't like your new dress. It brings out the gray in your hair." Or better still: "Junior, that's the ugliest drawing I ever saw, but please don't let that hurt your self-esteem."

But in our efforts to avoid offending someone, most of us overdo it. We are *too* timid, *too* hypocritical. Like politicians, we tend to say exactly what people want to hear—most of us, that is.

Every now and then someone breaks out of this mealy-mouthed mold, this going along to get along. Within the church certain names spring to mind: Martin Luther, Thomas More, Dietrich Bonhoeffer, Roger Williams, Martin Luther King, Jr., and now, James Dunn.

I first visited with James in his office overlooking the Capitol in 1985. I had on my best suit and was struggling mightily to make a good first impression. I was vying to become the Baptist Joint Committee's chief legal counsel. But James wasn't trying to impress anybody. He had on a vintage suit from J. C. Penney. When he accidentally dropped a nickel on the floor and it rolled under the table, he got down on his knees and picked it up.

This guy was different. I knew James had been president of Bread for the World and a voice for progressive causes in the arch-conservative Southern Baptist Convention. I had known my share of limousine liberals—bleeding hearts who enjoyed championing the cause of the poor and oppressed from their usual table at the country club. Odds were James was just another overblown preacher with little to back up his high-sounding words.

Wrong. During the eight years I served as his general counsel, James proved himself to be exactly what I had not expected: real.

James Dunn has been called many things: saint, scoundrel, genius, fool, banty rooster, a chihuahua who thinks he's a German Shepherd, a lion trapped in the body of a house cat. But I have another word for James, a word no one embodies quite like he: Baptist.

Asked to define what that means, James will flash a smile and sum up three centuries of Baptist theology like this: "Ain't nobody gonna tell me what to believe!"

But jokes aside, few understand as well as James what it means to be Baptist. Although he has spoken or written on scores of complex issues, each of his positions is rooted in his convictions about the very nature of God. James likes to say that being created in the image of God means being both free and responsible. "*Response-*

able," he would put it. "People come to God *freely* or not really," I have heard James say. Because God gives us the *freedom* to say "no" even to Him, we must not deny that same freedom to others. Not because we agree with, or even *like*, Hindus, Rastafarians, Atheists, or Wiccans. But because God demands it. That's why James opposes state-sponsored prayer in public schools or public support for parochial schools. It violates this fundamental Baptist tenet of soul liberty. Understand that, and you understand James Dunn.

The late Baptist great, T. B. Maston, ethicist *par excellence*, loved his gritty former student. The son of a poor Texas milkman, James would graduate from Southwestern Baptist Theological Seminary, then go on to complete his Ph.D. at the prestigious London School of Economics. Maston liked James' spunk. But spunk doesn't even begin to describe James Dunn.

In an age of nuclear giants and moral midgets, James Dunn stands like a redwood tree. At a time when the Southern Baptist Convention was being taken over by a cabal of self-appointed cardinals, I always knew there was one who would never bend the knee, who would accept no parachute, no matter how golden. Put it like this: If I were writing a dictionary for Baptists, under the word "courage," I would say simply: "See James Dunn."

When Ronald Reagan dared propose a constitutional amendment to allow government to sponsor religious exercises in public schools, James accused the popular president of "despicable demagoguery, playing petty politics with prayer." As for Lamar Alexander and his vouchers for private and parochial schools, James said they were "reckless, regressive, irresponsible, ill-conceived, expensive, harmful to the public school, elitist, and unconstitutional.... Other than that, they're OK!"

James Dunn is an equal opportunity offender. When a Democratic president appointed an ambassador to the Vatican, James was there to call his hand. I used to worry that this stressful life would kill James.

"James," I said, "You're going to get an ulcer."

"Buzz," he replied, "I don't get ulcers; I give them!"

One of my favorite recollections of James occurred at a meeting of the Executive Committee of the Southern Baptist Convention. Harold Bennett, executive secretary of the SBC ("top hired hand" as James would put it), had just returned from a meeting with the Pope. Dr. Bennett was reporting on his private meeting with the world's most esteemed member of the clergy. When the time came for questions, one of the newer members of the Executive Committee raised his hand. My ears perked up. "Did you share the gospel with him?" Dr. Bennett was dumbstruck. James, on the other hand, was amused. "Buzz," he said in a voice too loud to ignore, "genius has its limits, but ignorance knows no bounds!"

By contrast, James is one of the smartest men I have ever known. His intellect is more than academic, more than cognitive. It is emotional. He is able to connect with a wide audience of folk ranging from former Black Panthers to Sons of the Confederacy. You're likely to find James at the Metropolitan Opera or at Fort Worth's Fat Stock Show and Rodeo. Uptown, downtown, or small town; it really doesn't matter to James.

Coupled with his considerable intellect is a deep and genuine piety that almost seems quaint. He prays in King James English. James reminds me of the old southern saw: "I don't smoke, I don't chew, and I don't go with girls who do!"

I have seen James loan large sums of money to bad credit risks and never mention it again. I have seen him close down the office so we could all go eat ice cream together when someone had a birthday. He will laugh with those who laugh and weep with those who weep, and he has done both with me.

I cannot say this about many people, but I can say it about James. If Jesus walked up to him and said, "Sell all that you have— *all* that you have—and give to the poor, then come and follow me," James would do it. I doubt he would even flinch.

James has become a hero to Baptists struggling to survive in a world bent on denying the Baptist distinctive of soul liberty. Across the globe, governments seem hell-bent on enforcing religious orthodoxy at whatever cost. Witness the bloodshed in Sri Lanka, Pakistan, Indonesia, and the Middle East. Even the so-called enlightened European democracies such as France and Germany are trying their best to stamp out new religious movements such as Jehovah's Witnesses or the Church of Scientology. Not James. Even a state-sponsored crèche at a Missouri city hall is viewed as a threat to genuine freedom. Never mind that James likes the crèche. It is the fact that government is endorsing it that raises his ire. His willingness to defend the rights of the least minority has led him to denounce any use of the government's coercive powers to promote the faith. James understands, as did that forgotten Baptist hero George W. Truett, that "Christ's religion needs no prop of any kind from any worldly source, and to the degree that it is thus supported is a millstone hanged about its neck!"[1]

Whether you agree with him or not, we lemmings need James Dunn. And, like Harry Truman, whatever popularity he sacrifices today is likely to be viewed differently through the eyes of history.

Here's my prediction: Fifty years from now, yea 150 years from now, when the Baptist faithful gather, when they list the champions of soul liberty and its corollary, the separation of church and state—Roger Williams, Isaac Backus, John Leland, J. M. Dawson—the name Dunn will ring out. And well it should. James Dunn has become one of America's greatest treasures and one of the church's guiding lights. Long live James Dunn, Baptist.

Note

[1]From a sermon delivered on the east steps of the U. S. Capitol, 16 May 1920, in connection with the annual meeting of the Southern Baptist Convention.

Singing "Beulah Land" at American Baptist Churches, U.S.A. Evangelism Conference, Washington DC, 1992: (from left) Oliver "Buzz" Thomas, James Dunn, Pat Rogers Horn, Gordon Northcutt (note bow ties)

Wit and Wisdom
Remembering James Dunn

Victor Tupitza

> Four things a man must learn to do,
> If he would make his record true;
> To think without confusion, clearly;
> To love one's fellowman, sincerely;
> To act from honest motives, purely;
> To trust in God and heaven, securely.

JAMES DUNN INCLUDED THOSE WORDS of noted Presbyterian pastor Henry Van Dyke in his first "Reflections" column in the January 1981 issue of _Report from the Capital._ Why he selected those lofty sentiments of a distinguished pastor, poet, and writer at the outset of his service and what value he attached to them remains best known to him. Yet, from his office in the shadow of the U.S. Capitol, he took those inspiring words beyond mere text on paper. He incarnated them in sensitively written articles, provocative editorials, and inspiring sermons; in acts of loving concern; and especially in his day-to-day demeanor—all validating his worthiness to have been entrusted with the leadership of the Baptist religious liberty agency. His approach to life and service testify to a "wholeness"—an integration of thought and action rooted in faith and fidelity to Jesus Christ—that marks both the man and his mission.

In his initial column of "Reflections," James referred to a "commandment for all seasons: 'love the Lord thy God with all thy heart, and with all thy soul, and with all thy mind, and with all thy strength.' " And in his own inimitable way he cautioned, "To love God with one's whole mind calls for more stewardship of brainpower than most of us can muster." He concluded: "The Christian commitment is not academic, theoretical or speculative." Rather, as James has stressed on more than one occasion, "deeply rooted commitment relies on an experiential relationship with Jesus Christ as Lord and Savior."

The ultimate source of James' deep and abiding commitment to religious liberty and its prerequisite, soul freedom, became evident during the years I worked with him. It was rooted in the One whom to love and to follow is to discover and to know ultimate freedom—God our Creator, Redeemer, and Sustainer. For James, faith must be a voluntary response to God's love and thus intensely personal. Coercion has no place in the work of the church, even as it has no place in the gospel of Jesus Christ. Can it not be concluded, then, that privacy and liberty are in effect indivisible soul mates?

James continually demonstrated an unusual capacity to rise to the highest demands of Christian leadership: as tutor, reflective thinker, and able strategist. He functioned not on the basis of superior knowledge or executive authority but on the understanding that he was but one pilgrim cautiously leading other pilgrims, all dependent upon the guidance of the Spirit of God.

As editor of *Report from the Capital,* and especially in the role of director of denominational relations, it was my pleasure to work with James in ways both routine and serendipitous, the latter yielding the most memorable and cherished experiences. I appreciated the many facets of his personality and administrative ability. For good reason he could be both kind and cranky, as he was during a time when the extreme conservative theological/political faction of the Southern Baptist Convention first wrought confusion among elected officials on Capitol Hill. I valued his willingness to work with his hands as well as his mind, as on occasion he and Marilyn would help get a mailing out on schedule. I learned from him by listening in conversation as he dealt with an allusive concept, finally capturing it and expressing it with extreme clarity. At other times I caught a glimpse of a private dimension of the man that only from time to time trickled out in his writing. And sometimes I stood somewhat agog at being introduced to a national figure from among the broad expanse of his personal friendships—Jim Lehrer, Edwin Newman, Doug Marlette and Bill Moyers among them.

"James, the inimitable," he has been called by more than one person who has heard him preach or lecture, or has followed him through his column in *Report from the Capital*. "In a league all by himself" is another assessment often heard, perhaps following a presentation he delivered on soul liberty as the font of religious freedom to a denominational audience or a gathering of support-ers. To be sure, his folksy, down-to-earth style of communication has great appeal. Although it is a style that flows out of his South-western heritage, more importantly its witness to Christian experience is long on substance and only then garnished with the wry wit and subtle humor to which many of us look forward.

From the pantheon of saints who through the years have car-ried the torch of religious liberty, Joseph Dawson, E. Y. Mullins, and T. B. Maston made lasting contributions to the development of James' thought. They are joined by two Baptist congressmen, Brooks Hays and Fred Schwengel, who reinforced lessons about courage and fidelity. Both men lost their House seats because of principle: racial integration in the case of Democrat Hays and opposition to state-required religion in the public schools for Republican Schwengel. Add to that the example of Dunn's father, a dedicated layman, who taught James early the love of God and the innate sanctity of every human being as a creature formed in the image of God and worthy of all love. Outstanding Baptist leaders, a devoutly Christian home, and his own unvarnished love for Christ and zeal for the cause of religious freedom are fused in this Christian, a man totally professional and totally human.

The reference to love must not be misunderstood. There is nothing saccharine about James or the New Testament love he practices. Even among religious types, the word is bandied about in a manner that has obscured its meaning and detracted from its seriousness. Genuine love, the *agape* of Christ and concern of the Apostle, is premised on personal, self-giving opportunities and relationship; not on a high-minded ideal such as religious liberty.

James has demonstrated that the capacity to love has something to say about environment and especially the working environment in which we spend a good portion of our lives. It is one reason conditions at the Washington office of the BJC reflect something of its theological purpose. James calls it "a hangout on Capitol Hill." For volunteers, interns, part-time workers, and constituents, he has made it a place where almost every stray can wander in and find a haven of acceptance among the collection of regulars. Pastors or denominational workers drop in for information, to greet an old friend or colleague, to let staff know of their support, or to offer encouragement during a difficult time. Among the wanderers, often with college or seminary degrees in hand, have been persons with literally no place to go and others in search of the grail of purpose to which they could entrust their talents. Dunn turned no one away. No one went out the door without a hike in their hopes and perhaps renewed conviction that God continues to work His will in all our lives.

One such memorable incident began with a phone call that was somewhat untypical. The voice, tentative and pained, inquired, "Is there any chance you have an opening?" Knowing there was not, but confident that James would welcome that plaintive caller, we invited the young man to drop by the office. Somehow James could pull funds out of a hat for short-term assignments. (I sincerely believe the hat often came from his own rack.) Paperwork, filing, and answering phones always needed doing. "Scut work" was the term used, but not pejoratively, to engage the time and interest of numbers of interns from the collegiate ranks. And that was how this young man spent an interim period in his life: lending a hand wherever he was needed while at the same time putting together the shards of his life. He has since gone on to earn a doctorate. Another talented youngster who "dropped in" for a brief period is now an outstanding associate editor of a Baptist state paper, and a third went on to earn a doctorate in church history. A young woman, working before entering law school, now practices law. There are scores of "young'uns," using James' word, from within our denominational family who shared a commitment to religious liberty and may have answered your telephone call, written a news story, or served you in other ways.

James exhibited a spirit of openness that welcomed volunteers who thought they had something to contribute or who wanted a hands-on experience in church-state affairs. Doctoral candidates in that field and even missionaries on furlough were among ones who participated to the degree their time permitted. Because of the mutual value of such an arrangement, James instituted a "scholars-in-residence" program. It gave these professionals a first-hand experience of the cooperative endeavor taking place among denominations and religious faiths as they seek to address the government on behalf of First Amendment guarantees and pro-tections. Adherence to the religious liberty task was the only requirement.

It was nonnegotiable for James. Early in his tenure, President Reagan called for a constitutional amendment plugging prayer in the public schools because "God should never have been expelled from America's classrooms." The issue was to become more divisive than unifying among Baptists, for both political and religious rea-sons. After the prayer measure failed in the Senate, an alternate solution gathered momentum. The U.S. Supreme Court had already ruled in a Missouri case, *Widmar v. Vincent* (1981), that where an "open forum" existed, college students could not be denied use of facilities for religious purposes when they were available for secular uses. Senator Mark Hatfield (R-OR) and Representatives Don Bonker (D-WA) and Carl Perkins, Sr. (D-KY) introduced a proposal based on that decision. In high schools where activity times already were in place—for example, student chess clubs, political clubs, art clubs, and the like—students would be permitted to exercise their right to meet for Bible study or other religious purposes. Their meetings were to be held at the same hour when other interest groups met, but unlike the others, activities for religious purposes were to be voluntary, student-initiated, and student-led, with a faculty member present only to ensure order and safety.

The Equal Access Act was approved by the House on a 337-77 vote and by the Senate on an 88-11 vote in the summer of 1984. For Perkins, a Baptist whose "dogged persistence" was not to be curtailed, albeit with no little prodding by BJC staff, Equal Access brought his illustrious political career to a conclusion. *Report*, in a tribute to Perkins upon his death only a week and one day after passage, quoted his assessment of the BJC's effort: "You Baptists must stay here all night talking to congressmen and letting your people know to call their representative." It was Perkins' view, as he stated it following enactment of Equal Access, that "this legislation will do great things for the morals of this nation."

James was impressed by a humorous anecdote Brooks Hays told in his book, *Politics Is My Parish*, about the importance of writing letters. It seems that "a helpless little mother in Arkansas wrote to her husband who was locked away in the penitentiary, asking 'When do I plant the potatoes?' He wrote back saying, 'Not yet, but whatever you do, stay out of the garden; that's where the guns are buried.' Her next letter to him revealed that the authorities had been reading his mail. She wrote, 'I don't understand it. Two constables, a deputy, and the sheriff came out here and dug up every inch of the garden.' He answered, 'Now things are ready;

plant the potatoes.' " After preparing his next column (in long hand) for publication, that title somehow morphed into "Potatoes Is My Parish." The BJC director advised, "We may not get that sort of instant [potatoes] results from our letter writing. Write any-how." Elected officials value constituent correspondence, especially while legislation is still being written.

Edified by the counsel of Hays and the encouragement of Hatfield and Perkins, James will listen patiently to those who criti-cize the BJC position on an issue once he senses they have not been exposed to the subtleties inherent in church-state separation. He has been known, however, to go into a "mild" rage when he hears a supposedly enlightened media pundit or a church or civic leader promote a blatant misunderstanding of the nature of these relationships and voice a biased interpretation of the First Amendment. He offers in correction:

> A good many folks still think the words "Christian" and "politi-cian" are mutually exclusive, and that "Baptist" and "lobbyist" are a contradiction in terms. I'm not apologetic about the govern-mental relation aspect of BJCPA work; the work of the BJC is political but not partisan. The issues lead [us] to engage in a cooperative endeavor with other religious bodies and not to political party identification.

Indeed, the faith communities that worked for passage of the Equal Access Amendment ranged from the National Association of Evan-gelicals to the National Council of Churches of Christ in America, with bodies such as the Methodists, Friends, and Presbyterians somewhere in between. Current Senate Majority Leader Trent Lott, then a member of the House where he supported Reagan's prayer amendment, said after the law was enacted, "This has truly been a bipartisan effort. Protection of constitutional freedom knows no partisan lines." Very interesting!

James saw the Equal Access project as "a principled approach to church-state issues," an approach that is "constant and shaped

[more] by history, doctrine, and a dedication to religious liberty than by political exigencies." He believes that "it takes more hope to engage the gears of government with a distinctly Christian assignment than it does to proclaim the gospel from the pulpit because one does not offer an invitation to see a visible response." Lest that be taken as a put-down of the pulpit, one must first be aware that it's a rare Sunday morning when James and Marilyn worship together at their local church, Calvary Baptist. She's usually in the choir loft; he's out in some pulpit preaching.

The very nature of the First Amendment, guaranteeing no establishment and the free exercise of religion, forces religious liberty advocates to walk the fine line delineated by the principle of church-state separation. The BJC and other advocates of separation often encounter the criticism that because of their opposition to nationally prescribed religion, secularism is replacing it as the dominant national influence. These critics believe that Bible reading and religious observances in the public schools are one answer to that threat. First Amendment scholar and Christian ethicist T. B. Maston was aware of that fear in 1968 when he wrote, "The threat of secularism to liberty and to the church and its freedom is particularly acute when and where it has become a religion."

When sectarian motive disregards the abundant freedom guarantees of the two religion clauses, proponents will get precisely what they seek to avoid. James wrote that "secularization is exactly what would happen to prayer if some folks had their way . . . prayer would be put in uniform and forced to do civil duty." At another time, in his folksy way, he calmly contended, "The God whom I worship and serve has a perfect attendance record, never absent or even tardy." To politicians who traffic in the canard that God has been taken out of the public schools, he advised, "Before talking like theologians . . . think twice about the nature of God." James found it ironic that the ones who "quaked at the danger of secularism were the very ones pushing for prayer in public schools, an ultimate secularization" of the kind Maston feared.

Joseph M. Dawson, the BJC's first executive director, called attention to a necessary distinction. While America has been a nation of Christians, he denied that it ever had been a "Christian nation." Instead, he replied to those who held that view, "America is a nation of free men with religious liberty guaranteed by the Bill of Rights. Dawson noted that separation of church and state doesn't mean separation of God from government, or separation of religion from politics, or separation of Christianity from citizenship." James adds, "It took a Supreme Court decision to remind us [that] churches have the same rights as secular groups of private citizens to take strong positions on public issues." On that basis, he rejects the notion that religion has been banned from the "public square," calling it both superficial and faddish.

It's not too difficult to see soul liberty and astute biblical awareness permeating so much of what James says. About soul freedom he wrote, "The spark of the Divine in all of us that prompts awe and adoration is the flame worth guarding and defending in every person. The poignant recognition that 'nothing human is alien to me' . . . moves me to intense indignation at the thought of religious liberty for anyone being limited or denied." Reinforcing those thoughts, "A smug arrogance mars the mind of those who presume to sit in critical judgment on the Word of God. What a lofty perch, what a remarkable vantage point one assumes in dogmatically telling other believers what must be said of Scripture without having yet practiced it."

James used to tease this editor about always having "just one question," so I volunteer one final thought relating to equivocation: that was not his style. In fact, James likes to quote ole Harry Truman, who used to say, "I'm tired of all these two-handed fellers; it's always 'on the one hand, but on the other . . .'" Like the former president, you will not find James straddling an issue, especially regarding our Baptist family but in particular our Baptist heritage, which he deeply feels is being short-changed. In that vein he wrote, "It is popular today to say I'm a Christian first, only secondarily a

Baptist. . . . Our religion came to us through particular people. The fleshed-out nation of Christian faith demands specificity."

Henry Van Dyke's credentials have long been established and recognized. Those of us fortunate to have broken bread with James Dunn or worshiped or labored at his side have experienced many of the things written above. So, the close of this essay imitates its beginning:

> Precisely the spark of the Divine in all of us that prompts awe and adoration is the flame worth guarding and defending in every person.

> —James Dunn

Baptist Joint Committee staff in 1981 (from left): Stan Hastey, Victor Tupitza, John Baker, James Dunn

"THAT'S JAMES DUNN OF THE BAPTIST JOINT COMMITTEE—WE CALL HIM "GARFIELD" BECAUSE HE ALWAYS LANDS ON HIS FEET."
JOE McKEEVER

A Champion of Press Freedom

Pam Parry

IT'S HARD TO IMPRESS ANYONE THESE DAYS. In a time of blood-thirsty paparazzi and salacious TV shows, the line separating Dan Rather and Jerry Springer continues to blur. In fact, sensationalism has become so ho-hum that the latest and greatest is replaced daily with tomorrow's hype. The net result? In this day of exaggeration and flamboyance, it's tough to talk about living legends with any sort of credibility. But I don't know how else to discuss James Milton Dunn. A hero, he is the Michael Jordan of Baptists who were born in this century. Yes, that's right. That means he has no peer. Nada. Not one.

That's not to say that he doesn't have flaws or that I'm looking back on my days at the Baptist Joint Committee with the rose-colored glasses that only time and distance can provide. James is as human as the rest of us, and I remember that this noble agency is a place of employment with some of the typical workplace foibles. But professionally speaking, I have never been more proud to have my name associated with any group of committed Baptists. And despite our collective human condition, the BJC staff never wavered from its principles or from its commitment to Christ. And James' leadership helped us stay the course.

But my comparison of Dunn to Jordan has nothing to do with perfection or the adulation of fans, although James has carved a niche in Baptist folklore with the likes of John Leland and Isaac

Backus. The parallels I see in Dunn and Jordan have to do with their competitive spirit and dominance of their arenas. They are winners. Jordan led the Chicago Bulls to multiple NBA championships, while Dunn's BJC was one of the few Southern Baptist Convention agencies left standing after a twenty-year civil war that smote its sister agencies. And the length of the two men's respective runs has enabled them to put their imprimatur on society.

Dunn's steadfast commitment to religious liberty and its essential corollary, the separation of church and state, has left an indelible mark on Baptist life and has secured freedoms for every American. No doubt, he will long be remembered for his tenacious defense of the first sixteen words of the Bill of Rights: "Congress shall make no law respecting an establishment of religion, or prohibiting the free exercise thereof." Baptists will never forget the insults and attacks he endured in defense of religious liberty. But for me, there's much more to his legacy. As a journalist, I most admire that he gives more than lip service to freedom of the press. It's his defense of the rest of the First Amendment that completes the picture for me.

I admit that when I first contemplated becoming a congressional correspondent for Baptist News Service, I was frozen by the thought of it. I couldn't see myself following in the footsteps of Barry Garrett, Stan Hastey, Kathy Palen, and Larry Chesser. No news organization or group of journalists was more respected in Baptist life, and frankly, I couldn't envision myself in that news shop. Fortunately for me, James could. He had an eye for potential even in its rawest form, and he helped cultivate it. Much of what I have accomplished today I credit to his belief in my ability, which led to incredible opportunities.

Because of James, I've been to the Oval Office and the Cabinet Room to interview President Clinton. He also introduced me to President George Bush, Coretta Scott King, former Chief Justice Warren Burger, Vice-President Al Gore, TV commentator Bill Moyers, Senator Mark Hatfield, Pulitzer Prize winners, and the list goes on. As a journalist, I saw the civil rights legend Thurgood Marshall step down from the highest bench in the land; I saw Clarence Thomas square off against Anita Hill; and I saw Russian President Boris Yeltsin speak to the U.S. Congress for the first time in history. I covered a presidential inauguration, bill signings at the White House, State of the Union addresses, confirmation hearings for three Supreme Court justices, and oral arguments before the U.S. Supreme Court. My greatest professional moments I owe to James.

But my deep respect for the Texan doesn't stem solely from gratitude, but rather from a shared belief in a free and unfettered press. If any Baptist executive is a friend to the press, it is James Dunn. Unlike typical bureaucrats, he trusts the journalists on the BJC staff.

To the best of my memory, James and I only conflicted once in $4^{1}/_{2}$ years over the issue of how to cover the news. I barely remember the specific details. But we disagreed over whether to include additional material in a story I was sending to Associated Baptist Press. Like others who deal with the media, James felt strongly that I should include the material, a view he communicated with some zeal. He has a daunting personality. But being a person of similarly strong convictions, I disagreed. I was firm in my belief that the material could be construed as promotional and had no place in my story. After a taut exchange, James walked away, and we released the story without his suggestions. I felt good about the incident, not because James let me win, but because our shared value of press freedom prevailed. That man walks what he talks. Few people with comparable power to impose their will would decline to do so, but when it came to Baptist News Service, James opted not to do so on a daily basis. James is as much a champion of press freedom as he is a champion of soul freedom.

I appreciated the fact that James liked the press and understood our role in society. Even though he is a public figure in Baptist life, James loves to talk to reporters, and he has cultivated professional relationships with members of the Washington press corps. He believes most reporters will give him a fair shake, and I love him for that. Too often, people in Washington view the press as a necessary evil, something that won't go away, like a pesky dog barking in the middle of the night. But James understands that the press is an essential component for the continuation of a vital democracy. He views reporters as public servants who help empower private citizens with information. He sees reporters as trustees of the public and as his friends.

His relationship with reporters was evident every time the BJC would sponsor an editors' briefing. I was always impressed with the roster of high-profile media types who would attend the briefings for Baptist editors. In 1992 the BJC held a briefing in conjunction with its board meeting, an enriching experience I'll never forget. Pulitzer-prize-winning cartoonist Doug Marlette shared some of his finest work from *New York Newsday*. Joining the illustrious Marlette was NBC newsman Edwin Newman, former presidential press secretary Jody Powell, and Associated Press Supreme Court reporter Richard Carelli.[1] As a young journalist, I was impressed that so many top-notch journalists would share the wealth of their knowledge simply because they'd received an invitation from the BJC.

But I shouldn't have been surprised; relationship-building is one of James' spiritual gifts, and perhaps even the key to his legacy. He makes every person he meets feel special. He has an uncanny memory for minutiae when it comes to meeting people for the first time. Often he would introduce a visitor to the office, adding some tidbit about when, how, and under what conditions they first met. Sometimes he would remember what his friend had been wearing —down to the color and design of the clothing. Sometimes he would remember the weather conditions under which they met. Almost always he could recount the dialogue of the conversation they had shared. And he never forgot a name or person, making him or her feel like royalty.

The BJC staff tried to emulate this aspect of his personality. We learned that when we attended meetings it was important to pay attention to whom we might meet and to know something about them. People are impressed when you have taken the time to learn about them. But none of us had James' gift, which I think stems from his deepest Baptist innards. James wholeheartedly believes in the priesthood of the believer and the notion that "the ground is level at the foot of the cross." Despite his scholarship, accomplishments, and stature in the denomination, James has always seen himself as a servant whose constituents are the real heroes. He values every Baptist minister and layperson alike. He loves people, and when he meets someone for the first time, his enthusiasm radiates.

Before going to Washington, I was associate editor of the *Baptist True Union*, the weekly state Baptist newspaper in Maryland and Delaware. The first time I met him, James won me over because he'd read my work and thought highly of the newspaper. As a reporter, I was used to people saying they'd read my work as a way of ingratiating themselves to me, but James was different. He began to recount stories I had written and editorials by my editor Bob Allen. Wow. I was impressed. The next time I saw him was at the annual SBC meeting. He was chatting with a handful of SBC agency executives when he caught sight of me from the corner of his eye. I was walking past the group, and he paused his conversation to come over and shake my hand and tell me what a great reporter I was. We both knew it wasn't true, but it was nice of him to say so, and I felt special hearing it. I remember walking away struck by his generosity and his friendly demeanor and by the fact that he had stopped a conversation with arguably the most "important" people within the SBC to greet someone he had met only once before. A few years later, when James expressed interest in hiring me for the BJC staff, that incident alone influenced my decision. I wanted to work for a man who, even as a virtual stranger, could make me feel so validated.

But James doesn't just have a terrific manner with the everyday person; his relationship skills also serve him well with the movers and shakers in Washington, D.C. His compassion and experience in the nation's capital taught James that perhaps the famous and the powerful actually need support and friendship more than the average citizen. Lawmakers and politicians are always under intense pressure and assault from the latest person trying to unseat them. And James understands that fame and power do not insulate them from pain, pressure, and stress. He believes the ground is level at the cross for them, too.

Because of his compassion and integrity, James struck up friendships with several prominent lawmakers. He was a loyal friend, and they knew they could count on him. I remember observing his friendship with former Oregon Senator Mark Hatfield, who is Baptist. When I went for my job interview at the BJC, it culminated with a pizza party in the BJC library with Senator Hatfield as the guest of honor. Obviously, the senator hadn't come to see me, but the fact he was there having lunch with us after my interview made the experience truly memorable. When I returned to the *Baptist True Union*, I told Bob Allen about the interview and about having pizza with Hatfield. With his usual wit, Bob quipped something like, "How can I compete with that?"

But I hadn't seen anything yet. My greatest memory would come on the evening before the 1993 inauguration of President Bill Clinton and Vice-President Al Gore. The 1992 election of Clinton and Gore meant that, for the first time in U.S. history, two Southern Baptists would serve as president and vice-president. Although the Clinton-Gore ticket had its share of fans and detractors within Baptist ranks, James was excited about having a president and vice-president who would understand the historic Baptist belief in separation of church and state. So, he wanted the administration to begin with a Baptist blessing.

Along with Everett Goodwin, pastor of Washington's First Baptist Church, James set about planning an inaugural eve prayer service for the Clintons and Gores. He wanted both couples to attend—on a night typically devoted to glitzy pre-inaugural celebrations—and he hoped former president and fellow Southern Baptist Jimmy Carter could make it, too. For the first time out loud, I have to admit I thought James was nuts. How in the world was he going to persuade the Clintons and the Gores to leave the planned festivities with Hollywood celebrities and come to church the night before they were sworn into office? How would he get Jimmy Carter, Bill Moyers, Barbara Jordan, and a host of other dignitaries to come? He was good, but, come on, these people were busy preparing to run the country.

Boy, was I wrong. I underestimated James. And I'm ashamed to say, I underestimated the Clintons and the Gores. They seemed touched that 1,000 Baptists wanted to gather on January 19, 1993, and pray for them twelve hours before they took the oath of office.[2] When the Clintons and Gores cascaded down the aisles of First Baptist Church in Washington, I remember thinking, "Where else would committed Christians want to be the night before taking on the biggest responsibility of their lives?" For the record, Carter, Moyers, Jordan, and a host of others also attended the prayer service.

Although many people worked hard to pull off this jointly-sponsored event, the BJC staff marveled at what James had done. We knew that without him, the prayer service would never have happened.

But that wasn't his greatest feat. To me, the legacy of James Dunn is the very survival of the BJC. During the twenty-year battle over control of the Southern Baptist Convention, the tiny religious liberty agency was battered and bruised from fundamentalist assaults. A new regime had ushered in a different kind of convention through the use of puppet presidents, and SBC agency heads were dropping like flies. James was the most hated target. His colorful rhetoric and unflinching courage made fundamentalists' blood boil. They wanted his proverbial head on a platter, and they would use any means to get it. They tried to pack the BJC board, but because of the other supporting Baptist bodies, the SBC fundamentalists were unable to gain control of the agency. Frustrated with that outcome, they turned to hounding and harassing the staff, particularly Dunn. They made life unhappy for other BJC board members and staffers alike. But finally, when they were convinced they could not win, the fundamentalists took their money and went home in 1991.

The cutting of SBC ties was the greatest gift the agency had received in terms of the freedom it allowed from the tyranny of an SBC-turned-hard-to-the-right. The new denominational leaders wanted the BJC to abandon principles for politics. But Dunn and company wouldn't budge.

I joined the agency shortly after the defunding, and in my mind the survival of the organization was very much in question. I wondered whether I would be dusting off my résumé in six months because the BJC might have to close its doors. But I took the gamble because I believed that right-thinking Baptists wouldn't let the agency die. Also, I knew that James was as tenacious as anyone, and he gave me his personal assurance that I would never miss a paycheck. He kept his word.

That's not to say that in the first two years following the SBC defunding things weren't tight, because they were. After I'd been on staff about six months, I remember contemplating a job move because I felt insecure. We had held a staff meeting at which James had instructed us to refrain from buying so much as a pen without his approval. That scared me—until I realized that James' penny-pinching ways were going to help the agency not just survive, but thrive. A product of the Depression, James' frugality became a way of life even after things became comfortable again. And every paycheck came like clockwork, so I put out of my mind thoughts of desertion. Even if this roller-coaster ride ends, I thought to myself, I don't want to stop before the next corner.

Through James' leadership, vision, frugality, and relationship to numerous Baptists, funding poured in that outweighed the former SBC contribution. His friends, colleagues, and fans kept the BJC alive and have helped it thrive once again. His knack for friendship translated into tremendous fundraising, and the BJC stands poised for the new millennium stronger than ever. Perhaps no other person in any other time could have pulled it off but James Milton Dunn.

Notes

[1]Mark Wingfield, "Dramatic Year Seen for Court, Congress," *Report from the Capital* (November-December 1992): 5.

[2]Bob Allen, "Praying Baptists: Clintons, Gores Join in Inaugural Eve Service" *Report from the Capital* (February 1993): 10, 14.

Pam Parry

Barbara Jordan and James Dunn at the 50th Anniversary Celebration, First Baptist Church, Washington DC, October 1986

President Bill Clinton and James Dunn in the White House, January 1997

Sail On, O Ship of Faith!

—— *Marvin C. Griffin* ——

IN THE AFRICAN AMERICAN SPIRITUAL, the "Old Ship of Zion" is
in life's dark sea. The Captain calls out loud to those free to come
and be saved. The ship sails through contrary winds and confronts
the threat of shipwreck, but in the end, it weathers every storm.
Thomas Dorsey decribes the call and response:

> Then I stepped aboard the vessel
> Thro' the straights and thro' the gorge,
> Many years it sailed the waters
> Many souls have made the voyage.

Unlike King Jehoshaphat's ships in Ezion-Geber that never
sailed because they were destroyed in the harbor, the ship of the
Baptist Joint Committee has been in the water, going from port to
port. Like a ship tossed and driven on tempestuous waters, the BJC
has had several captains to guide it safely from harbor to harbor. As
a passenger on the ship for almost two decades, I welcome the
opportunity to describe the resulting insights and experiences that
have inspired me and shaped my life.

I cannot really recall when and where I met James Dunn. It
seems he was always there, waiting to reach out to others in peace,
justice, and love. He was there, rising above the artificial barriers of
race and region; beyond the paths of provincialism and parochial-

ism and the schemes of partisan politics. At such a time as this, when voices are crying in the wilderness, the wilderness is crying for a voice. Our generation longs for a voice above the cries of civil religion, the voice of truth, a priestly and prophetic voice that articulates and interprets human needs.

The Baptist Joint Committee's search for such a voice led to James M. Dunn, who was director of the Christian Life Commission of the Baptist General Convention of Texas. I came to know James nearly thirty years ago when I became a member of the Commission.

For three decades, James Dunn has engaged in a lover's quarrel with government over issues of social justice. It has been more than a quarrel; it has been a fierce struggle in which the antagonists have returned to the battlefield time and time again with fresh forces, new resources, and renewed determination. With its limited resources, the Baptist Joint Committee has been like little David facing the giant Goliath.

In some ways James Dunn has been a trailblazer, a pioneer making new paths for future travelers. In some ways he has been a bellwether, sounding the alarm and giving directions to the flock of God. He has been a fearless leader during times when fearless leaders are as scarce as hen's teeth.

I am profoundly impressed by Dunn's openness and courage in confronting social justice issues at times when it was unpopular to do so. I first became familiar with the work of the Texas Christian Life Commission during the tenure of A. C. Miller in the 1940s. In those days the Southern Baptist Convention's prophetic social justice commission was known as the Social Service Commission. I recall recommendations made to the Convention during those years. They included calling African Americans "Mr." and "Mrs." This particular recommendation infuriated some members of the Convention.

Texas was one of the leading states among Baptists in addressing social issues, preparing and circulating materials, and providing program services for churches. James Dunn carried on this prophetic tradition established by Miller and his successors Foy Valentine and Jimmy Allen.

From this background, rich in opportunity and experience, James Dunn was selected as executive director of the Baptist Joint Committee. It was a giant step from Dallas to Washington, from a state convention commission to a national committee representing the major Baptist bodies of the United States.

As an aside note, before his departure to the East, the church of which I am pastor, Ebenezer Baptist in Austin, Texas, invited James and his lovely wife, Marilyn, to be our guests during Sunday morning worship. James was to deliver the sermon, and Marilyn was to sing. Virgie Carrington DeWitty, the minister of music, nationally known as a composer and singer of gospel music, coached Marilyn, encouraging her to add notes in typical African American style—a departure from what she had learned from her father, a music professor at Southwestern Baptist Theological Seminary for many years. Marilyn's solo was outstanding, a delight to the congregation. If she had remained with us longer, we may have succeeded in making her a distinguished "Anglo-African-American" gospel singer.

The Baptist Joint Committee is the Washington-based watchdog for Baptists in church-state matters. Since its beginning, the Christian faith has suffered hostility and oppression when the relationship between church and state has been too tight. Jesus Christ, author and finisher of our faith, suffered unjustly under Pilate, the Roman governor. The authorities tried to entrap Jesus with tricky questions concerning religion and the state:

"Is it lawful for us to give tribute unto Caesar, or no?" But [Jesus] perceived their craftiness and said unto them, "Why tempt ye me? Shew me a penny. Whose image and superscription hath it?" They answered and said, "Caesar's." And He said unto them, "Render therefore unto Caesar the things which be Caesar's and unto God the things which be God's." (Luke 20:22-25, KJV)

In the early days of the church, two apostles responded to a dilemma with the words, "We ought to obey God rather than men." Paul used his Roman citizenship to advance his missionary endeavors. He admonished Christians to "be subject for the Lord's sake to every human institution, whether it be the emperor as supreme, or to governors as sent by him to punish those who do wrong and praise those who do right."[1] In 1 Peter 4:4, written during a time when Christians were suffering persecution, believers are encouraged to be happy if reproached for the name of Christ. God is glorified by such behavior.

Baptists have made a unique contribution to American life through belief and practice concerning church-state relations. John Bennett says,

> There is no Protestant doctrine concerning church/state relations. There is a Baptist doctrine that is very clear and that has always had great influence in this country. There is an American doctrine which has been developing since the beginning of the Republic and some aspects of it are still being clarified by the courts.[2]

Baptists have always been opposed to all ties between church and state and have suffered religious persecution under state churches because of their unwavering and uncompromising stand.

Receiving the torch from his predecessors, James Dunn has continued this noble tradition. His high-pitched voice mounts to a mighty crescendo when he says that the state should not interfere with the church's realm: "The state should keep their cotton-picking hands off it." He has given the major portion of his life to helping America live up to the promise stated in the Constitution: "Congress shall make no law respecting an establishment of religion, or prohibiting the free exercise thereof."

America's system of church-state separation results not from hostility to Christianity or from a desire to put churches at a disadvantage. It is the result of the conviction and belief that churches are better off on their own.

Stephen Carter claims that in recent years our nation has run a serious risk of breaching the wall of separation between church and state and that, for the past several decades, our courts have misinterpreted the First Amendment. Civil religion has appeared on the horizon of our faith. America's religious traditions are invoked in support of partisan politics.

Baptists know from experience the value of religious freedom because of the persecution we suffered at the hands of established religion. Our heritage includes a long list of martyrs who suffered and died in the struggle for religious freedom. From colonial America we have such brave soldiers as Roger Williams, John Clarke, Thomas Painter, Henry Dunster, Obadiah Holmes, and Thomas Goold. Martin Luther King Jr., a modern social prophet, continued that tradition. This precious birthright of religious freedom is not for sale at any price. Every person must be free to worship God according to the dictates of his own conscience. As the words of a hymn tell us,

> Let Caesar's dues be paid
> To Caesar on his throne.
> Conscience and the soul were made
> To belong to God alone.

America needs the prophetic voice of the Baptist Joint Committee as a constant reminder of the constitutional guarantee concerning religious liberty. We need this constant reminder lest we forget that God is the Creator and we are the creatures. God is not the servant of the state; the state is an order of God's creation.

I have been a member of the Baptist Joint Committee during most of the nineteen years James Dunn has served as executive director. During the earlier years James exhibited great passion over aid to parochial schools. He was not caught in the controversy regarding whether or not Catholicism would win America; his concern was about the use of state public funds for private schools sponsored by religious groups. He strongly believes that these institutions should provide their own funds and not depend on government action and grants. Aid to parochial schools was the burning issue when James Dunn assumed the helm of the Baptist Joint Committee. It is still an issue today—in the form of school vouchers. Labels have changed, but the basic issue remains the same. If government tinkers with our religious liberty, we run the risk of losing our freedom.

As the issues sharpened and opposition became more intense, allies of the Baptist Joint Committee were attacked and funds regarded as the foundation of its support were first reduced and finally withdrawn. But personal attacks and false accusations have not caused the BJC to waiver from its steadfast loyalty to separation of church and state. James Dunn has been a fearless leader through all the trials and tribulations. He has garnered support where he could, even where it triggered criticism, controversy, and conflict from some elements of his own Southern Baptist constituency.

When aid from the Southern Baptist Convention was cut off, support from state conventions, churches, and individuals increased. Through the years, support for the Baptist Joint Committee has been expanded and strengthened so that it once again is strong and secure.

Just as the Baptist witness prospered under persecution in the past, so the prophetic voice of the Baptist Joint Committee is louder and more effective than ever. Because of this voice crying in the wilderness, modern-day Pharisees and Sadducees have gathered in the region and experienced a new understanding of the application of the doctrine of separation of church and state in belief and practice.

It is imperative that the voice in the wilderness continues to cry and be heard. More religious groups in America are becoming devotees of partisan politics and prisoners of single issues unknowingly, sacrificing religious liberty and freedom of conscience in the process. Baptists can be grateful that the voice of the Baptist Joint Committee has not been silenced by its persecution. Its stalwart witness in the face of danger and difficulty deserves high praise. Our Lord said:

> Blessed are ye, when men shall revile you, and persecute you, and shall say all manner of evil against you falsely, for my sake. Rejoice, and be exceeding glad: for great is your reward in heaven: for so persecuted they the prophets which were before you. (Matt 5:11-12, KJV)

The Baptist Joint Committee has not sought to espouse popular positions. It has often taken unpopular, even controversial, positions. During World War II, the BJC issued a statement against the indiscriminate condemnation of all American citizens of Japanese ancestry based on assumed links between them and those responsible for outrageous executions of American aviators. The report read:

> As representatives of church organizations which have been working for many years with Japanese in America, we desire to make public record of our conviction that no blanket condemnation of all American citizens of Japanese ancestry is in any sense justified. We are convinced that loyalty to American democratic ideals and aversion to the purpose and practices of Imperial Japan among these American citizens of Japanese ancestry is comparable to that of other groups of American citizens and that they are patriotically desirous of the overthrow of the Axis powers for the sake of the peace of the world. We desire and declare our confidence in the competency of our government to discover and restrain all traitorous and subversive elements which exist among Japanese in the United States and its territories, differentiating between those that are loyal and those that are disloyal to our country. We likewise affirm it as our conviction that instead of aiding our government in this necessary

undertaking, those who call upon the government to deny all civil rights to American citizens of Japanese ancestry are playing into the hands of the powers that are fighting against us by adopting their point of view in regard to race in abrogating certain fundamental tenants of our democracy. (Adopted at a regular meeting of the Committee on Public Relations, Washington, D.C., 27 April, 1943.)[3]

People who grew up when America was predominantly Protestant often find it difficult to accept cultural pluralism. The 1962 decision forbidding use of a form of prayer in schools may be the single most controversial Supreme Court decision. It has certainly received a cold reception in the South. Legislatures have considered numerous bills designed to nullify the ruling. But the prayer decision preserves religious liberty. In reality, no one can keep another from praying. Prayer is personal communication with God. In the words of the hymn,

> Prayer is the soul's sincere desire
> uttered or expressed
> The motion of a hidden fire
> that trembles in the breast.

The state should engage in no action to promote religion. Neither should it prohibit the growth of religion. The Baptist Joint Committee does not seek the return of the Holy Roman Empire, nor does it wish to see a situation of complete state domination where religion is crushed, as in Russia. Rather, it seeks healthy coexistence with neither church nor state dominating. A free church in a free state is the desire of religious liberty advocates. Dietrich Bonhoeffer summarized the role of the state thus:

The state serves to protect man from the invasion of chaos and therefore gives him time: time for the preaching of the Gospel; time for repentance; time for faith. Since according to the measure of human insight and human capacity and under the threat and exercise of force, provision is made in the state for the establishment of human law and the inevitably external, relative, and provisional sense for freedom and peace and humanity, it renders a definite service to Divine Providence and the plan of salvation, quite apart from the judgment and desires of its members.[4]

As we confront a new millennium, we face a wave of increasing intolerance by both religious and government actors. For example, an Alabama judge disregards the law and places the Ten Commandments on the wall of the courtroom, and religious groups bomb abortion clinics. Freedom involves not only the right to exist but *to be*. The church is not to be a captive of the community. Neither is the community to be a captive of the church. Each must be free to pursue its God-given function without pressure or oppression.

James Dunn dignifies and glorifies our cherished tradition of freedom by his distinguished service to Baptists and the nation. He has gathered around him an efficient and dedicated staff who carry on the work at great sacrifice. He has weathered the storm that threatened to destroy the ship. He has brought the ship safely into port. Now it is the task of another captain to sail the uncharted seas of the future. The ship is larger and better equipped to carry more cargo than the one James inherited, but the goal remains the same: to preserve and protect religious freedom.

The advice and counsel of the Baptist Joint Committee has been recognized, sought, and appreciated in the highest government circles. It has remained faithful to Baptist principles and its mission. Without compromise or rancor, the ongoing debate has been conducted with integrity and courageous action.

President Harry Truman said, "A leader has to lead or . . . he has no business in politics." In working with representatives of Baptists in North America and the judicial, legislative, and executive branches of our government, James Dunn has demonstrated the brightest and best qualities of Christian leadership.

Arnold Toynbee, the renowned English historian, says history is made of two forces: challenge and response. The challenge is always before us. The church will constantly face the issue of how it should relate to the state while striving to remain separate and free. The goal of Baptists is a free church in a free state.

Yesterday is history. On the edge of a new millennium the Baptist Joint Committee is summoned to respond to the challenge of writing a new history. Another captain will assume the helm, and the voyage will continue until that day when the kingdoms of this world become the kingdoms of our Lord and Christ (Rev 11:15).

Notes

¹John Bennett, *Christians and the State* (New York: Charles Scribner's Sons, 1958) 30.

²Ibid., 205.

³William H. Brackney. *Baptist Life and Thought: 1600-1980* (Valley Forge PA: Judson Press, 1983) 4274.

⁴Karl Barth. *Christian Community and Civil Community* in *Against the Stream* (New York: Philosophical Library, 1954) 22.

Marvin Griffin, BJC Board meeting 1998

A Darned Good Churchman
—— Lynn A. Bergfalk ——

IT WAS A MOMENT OF DEEP FEELING and reflection for Baptist Joint Committee board members when James Dunn, at our October 1998 meeting at Green Lake, Wisconsin, told us that he would be stepping aside from his role as executive director. For many of us, the Baptist Joint Committee and James Dunn seemed inseparable. Even a transition that continued a part-time role for James at the BJC would require a readjustment in our mental universes.

"For me, religious liberty and the separation of church and state have had a face, and it's always been your face," said Julie Pennington-Russell, a Texas pastor, reflecting younger Baptists' experiences.

My own feelings of gratitude and affection for James were magnified by being his pastor for the past five years. However, God paints on a big canvas. I have never been quite sure whether we ought to date our relationship with James to when he joined Calvary Baptist in 1994 or trace it to 1907, when the Northern Baptist Convention was organized in our sanctuary with New York governor Charles Evans Hughes, later Chief Justice of the Supreme Court and active Calvary member for thirty-six years, served as its first president. Allow me to explain.

Hughes, a distinguished statesman who twice just missed the presidency of the United States, wrote a classic dissenting opinion as Chief Justice in 1931 that said religious or conscientious scruples

should not constitute a disqualification for citizenship. The case involved the proposed naturalization of a Canadian citizen who resided in the United States and refused to swear that he would bear arms in defense of the country.

In 1931 there was no Baptist Joint Committee to address an issue of this kind. In the absence of such a vehicle, the Calvary congregation unanimously adopted a resolution supporting Hughes' dissenting opinion and urging passage of a bill pending in Congress that would prevent a person's opinion concerning war from being a test of fitness for citizenship. Historical perspective suggests this episode was just another of the brush strokes of a liberty-loving God already at work forming what would be a powerful and persistent Baptist voice for religious liberty in our nation's capital.

If God paints on a big canvas, perhaps then it was no accident that also in 1931, off in Texas, a certain child was conceived. In the synchronicity of God's time, the formation of the Baptist Joint Committee in 1936 by the Northern Baptist Convention (now American Baptist Churches, USA) and the Southern Baptist Convention surely grasped the whole of the twentieth century, not only events and people who brought it to birth, but also the leader who would guide it through the turbulent years at the end of the century.

Of course, we can never step back far enough from the canvas to take in the whole sweep. While at Calvary we have a visceral sense of those larger but mostly unseen linkages, our picture of James Dunn is up close and personal. A Texas story, via the dairy farm I grew up on in Minnesota, captures our Calvary perspective on James.

My dad used to tell how our neighbor Clarence was driving his John Deere tractor in a hayfield when a big Cadillac with Texas license plates came down our gravel road. The driver saw Clarence, pulled over, and struck up a conversation.

"I'm a rancher," the fellow said, "and I'm curious about how much cattle and land you folks have up here."

"I've got twelve cows," Clarence responded, "and my place runs from that barn over there to the fence row behind us." And then, trying to be polite, "How big is your ranch?"

The Texan smiled. "You might find this hard to believe, but I can get in my pickup in the morning and still not get to the other side of my spread by sundown."

"Shucks, I understand that," a sympathetic Clarence assured the rancher. "Had a truck like that once myself."

Here in Washington, Calvary Baptist knows the dairy-farm, local-church-sized James Dunn, the friendly guy with the bow tie who doesn't get to church nearly as often as his wife Marilyn, who is unfailingly faithful in the choir, for all his preaching elsewhere.

Many of us also know the Texas-sized, larger-than-life champion of religious liberty who tenaciously has led the Baptist Joint Committee through the tumultuous challenges of the past decade or two. But knowing Brother James as part of a local church may give us something a little different to add to the tributes offered upon his retirement as the BJC's executive director.

We can attest to the congruence between the public persona and the regular guy who shows up at church, the consistency between the principles articulated on the national stage and their grassroots application, the continuity between James' passionate stand on issues and his personal commitment to Christ and the church. We can affirm a kindness and a concern for others in the off-stage living that reflects James' motto, "Do good by stealth and be discovered by accident." He quietly and consistently goes out of his way to help and to open doors for others, especially for young people who need that extra boost to get started.

Few of us probably understand the workload behind James Dunn's devotion to the cause of religious liberty or how unselfishly and tirelessly he has worked to fulfill that calling on behalf of the Baptist Joint Committee. Just keeping up with the complexities of current church-state issues requires exhaustive reading and immense intellect and energy. Throw in the endless travel, meetings, speeches, writing, and all the rest, and it takes a saintly wife and the willingness to eat, breathe, and sleep his work to meet the demands.

Given how consuming the job is, the momentous issues at stake, and the constant interaction with media and political and religious leaders, one might be tempted to ask, "What is the local church that James should be mindful of it?" But what we at Calvary find in James is a real Baptist who practices the stuff we teach in church membership and seminary polity classes about the importance of the local church.

"Unless folks understand that from the New Testament perspective references to 'church' are overwhelmingly related to the local church, specific congregations of particular flesh and blood human beings," James always insists, "they do not understand the New Testament message."

While it is true, he continues, that we are part of a larger spiritual family in Christ transcending all human dividing lines, "faithful engagement in the local church and the willingness to find one's niche is essential to practical Christianity."

That willingness was demonstrated to us in June 1994. The Dunns had visited Calvary several times, and we were pleased that James had accepted our invitation to speak on Religious Liberty Sunday. He preached with characteristic zest and wit and, when finished, extended an invitation to Christian discipleship. "Perhaps some of you," he added, "need a church home, and we would invite you to join this congregation. In fact, this is the kind of church Marilyn and I would like to be part of, and we're going to step down front as we sing the invitation hymn to present ourselves for membership at Calvary."

James and Marilyn really did join Calvary that day. He has never been too big or too busy to be an honest-to-goodness active member of the local church. He is not only a strong presence, but one who is there when you need him, supporting both program and staff. Somehow he even shoe-horned into his busy schedule the demanding commitment (and given our building and budget issues, it is demanding!) of serving as a trustee. And he has been good to his "pasture" (as he playfully calls the pastor on whom he generously claims to "feed"); our staff finds his genuine affection and encouragement a real boon.

Characteristically, James enjoys a little fun at his own expense, claiming he's not much of a church member, "just shows up Christmas and Easter" and a few times in between when he doesn't have "hired gun" assignments elsewhere. But then he grins: "I do send my tithe and my wife."

We're lucky that Marilyn stays home while James roams the country. When she joined Calvary, it was like adding staff and sunshine. She has a beautiful voice, and in addition to being devoted to the choir, she is always willing to provide special music. She serves on the mission board, keeps the women's organization going (whether serving as president or "just" as a member), and is the quintessential church volunteer investing hours wherever needed. No task is too small or too menial to be accepted with grace and done with dedication. James may be the salt of the earth, but there is something of the sweetness of heaven about Marilyn. She weaves together an unfailingly gracious spirit and positive attitude with unflagging zeal and the courage of her convictions.

At the heart of downtown Washington, Calvary is just a mile (and a couple of Metro stops) from the BJC office and the Dunns' Capitol Hill home. Their membership continues a strong history between the church and the Baptist Joint Committee. Since its inception, every senior minister at Calvary has served on the BJC board, and several BJC staffers have been members of the congregation. Other past members of Calvary, like Congressmen Brooks Hays and Fred Schwengel, were exemplars of Baptist principles in public life and strong supporters of the BJC.

James has referred to Hays, Schwengel, and Clarence Cranford as "megaphones of a long, profound, historic commitment to religious liberty at Calvary." Hays (D-AK) and Schwengel (R-IA) lost their seats in Congress, both after eight terms, as a result of their courageous stands on human rights and religious liberty issues.

In his September 9, 1997 "Reflections" column in *Report from the Capital*, James wrote on Brooks Hays as an example of how "a dedicated individual can redirect the flow of history." His lifetime devotion to civil rights and social justice was dramatically demonstrated in 1957 when he took a leading role in the integration of Little Rock Central High School. In one of the interesting quirks of Calvary's history, he also served as president of the Southern Baptist Convention in 1958, the same year Calvary's pastor, Clarence Cranford, was president of the American Baptist Convention, and this was the first and only time the presidents of the two conventions came from the same congregation. Together they made a goodwill tour to Baptists in the Soviet Union, where they spoke in churches and expressed friendship to the people of the Soviet Union at the height of the Cold War.

Hays' commitment to racial justice and international understanding was not applauded by Arkansas voters, who turned him out of office in the 1958 elections. Fred Schwengel suffered the same fate in 1970 when he put principle before politics by opposing state-sponsored school prayer.

After leaving Congress, Schwengel remained in Washington as president of the United States Capitol Historical Society, whose offices are just a floor above the BJC's. A day at the BJC couldn't be considered complete until Fred dropped in to check on the staff. Brent Walker, the BJC's general counsel, recalls him "roaming the halls of the Baptist Joint Committee regaling us with stories, quoting poetry, and, when he couldn't remember the lines, he would pull them out of the virtual file cabinet he kept in his breast pocket."

A big bear of a man who recited his stories and poems in a booming voice with impressive rhetorical flourishes, "Fred" was an authentic American character who evidenced profound religious faith and deep love of country. Because both were so precious, Fred continued impassioned advocacy for the separation of church and state right to the end of his long and productive life.

Schwengal's passion for religious liberty was inseparable from his ardent support for Dunn and the BJC, especially as the agency came under fire from those whom Fred felt had either forsaken or forgotten their historic Baptist roots. In the years before the Dunns were at Calvary, Fred Schwengel made sure his church and his pastor remained informed and energized supporters. Many of my first impressions of James came through Fred—a good introduction, indeed.

On the humorous side, Fred once prevailed on James to publish a Baptist heritage calendar that he dreamed would educate rank-and-file church members in both history and religious liberty. Unfortunately, the calendars, sporting the stern visage of John Leland on the cover, never caught on, and the unsold stock became an inadvertent part of Fred's "lasting contribution" to the cause. However, the Baptist Joint Committee already had suitably honored this great friend in 1986, by bestowing on him one of the two first J. M. Dawson Religious Liberty Awards.

Despite the great names and memories of the past, Calvary has been defined over the years more by community ministry than by celebrity members. The oft-told story about how Pastor Samuel Greene welcomed Justice Hughes and a Chinese laundry worker into the church as they stood side by side at the front of the sanctuary with the words, "The ground is level at the foot of the cross," captures the essence of both the gospel and Baptist life.

Level ground more than illustrious history seemed to draw James and Marilyn Dunn to this urban church halfway between the White House and the Capitol, at the crossroads of privilege and poverty, influence and impotence. Its doors are open to the high and honored along with the homeless and hopeless, and its members reflect the cosmopolitan flavor of the city, crossing not only boundaries of race and culture, but also of social and economic class.

Among the diverse gathering on a Sunday morning are congregational stalwarts whose membership stretches over the decades, a growing number of internationals, a seasoning of young adults and families, and a somewhat boisterous knot of kids from our community programs who barely know the first thing about church manners and protocol. Whether by choice or by chance, James' habitual seat (on the right aisle, several rows from the front) borders these community kids.

"So far I've resisted all temptation to reach over and tap them and say, 'We don't talk in church,' " James recently told me. "But I did reach over and open the hymnal to the right page, handed it to the kids, and several began to sing!"

Paget Rhee, our director of youth and outreach, valiantly tries to maintain order and participation as she sits with these kids. She cringes as the wiggling and noise rise and fall, wondering how this display of license sits with that distinguished statesman of religious liberty just a pew or two removed. She confided her relief that, when she furtively murmurs, "Sorry, sorry," to James, he catches her eye with a smile and a wink of approval. After the service, he often assures her that she is "doing a great job" in her corner of the world.

Folks sometimes say to us at Calvary, "You're doing what we believe churches should do. Of course, it doesn't really fit where I am personally right now . . . but you have our admiration!"

James and Marilyn have not been admirers from afar. Instead, they give their time, attention, tithe, and enthusiastic endorsement to Calvary's community mission. "Wherever I go," James says, "I tell people I'm a member of the most dedicated missionary church I've been in during my forty-five years in ministry. We have more local mission involvement per square head than any church I've been part of."

The encouragement, support, and understanding James gives to his church's mission reflects the practical side of the principles he espouses. He believes there's a right way to do right, that churches don't need "charitable choice" legislation to roll up their sleeves and bring help and hope and healing to their communities. James champions ministries at Calvary, including programs for urban youth; meals and other services for the homeless; ESL classes; ministries with Latino, Burmese, and other international groups; and Urban Hands, which involves high school and college students in mission projects throughout the city.

As a church trustee, James has supported uses of our buildings that reflect a collaborative vision for the shalom of the city: a YWCA day-care center, For Love of Children school for at-risk youth, an employment support center, offices for other community organizations, and meetings for twelve-step groups and Habitat for Humanity volunteers.

As a downtown church, Calvary has transitioned from a storied past to the humbler role of serving the poorest and most vulnerable members of society. James speaks approvingly of "the forty different things going on that show how utterly committed we are to the community in which we live."

He sometimes adds that these extensive activities flourish without assistance or entanglement from any government agency. Religious organizations don't need access to tax dollars to fulfill their mission. We're committed to doing what we can with what we have in our own way and to partnering with others in the community as we see fit in a holistic approach that integrates the social and spiritual dimensions.

His encouragement of this model of ministry reflects the congruence of principle and practice that is characteristic of James. Even if his praise is more generous than I think we deserve, he makes us (to borrow from Jack Nicholson in *As Good As It Gets*) want to be a better church!

Incarnating faith and values at the nitty-gritty local level empowers the broader application of principles of liberty and justice. James connects with the tradition of the Hebrew prophets, who were part of the people, not prima donnas seeking the limelight of power and prestige. They were reluctant mortals thrust forward by the Spirit and compelled by conscience to speak to issues that demanded attention. They were not politicians with a finger to the wind of popular opinion, or pragmatists who allowed circumstances to trump the Truth. They were radical, not in forsaking the past, but in reclaiming their roots, in translating tradition into the contemporary idiom. They remembered the rock from which they were hewn.

Real Baptist polity leaves little room for celebrity preachers or talking heads, but preserves and even calls forth the prophetic role. Both his homespun, unpretentious manner and his stubborn, impassioned, uncompromising message have marked James Dunn as a modern-day prophet in and beyond Baptist circles. The fact that, in championing the cause of religious liberty James has never outgrown the local church is a mark of his authenticity. There is inherent humility in supporting the priesthood of all believers and in being part of a local body, warts and all, that works and witnesses in the world.

James also models the courage, conviction, and integrity that empowered the prophets of old to confront a people who had trivialized the faith of the exodus into a civil religion that domesticated God in support of the status quo. A religion of rituals and propositions assumes God can be manipulated to perform so long as we merely put our pieces in their proper places.

The prophets cut through this cheap God-in-a-box piety that pretended to provide what God supposedly wants, reminding folks that they already knew the good that God expected. "What does the Lord require of you but to do justice, to love kindness, and to walk humbly with your God?" (Micah 6:8).

In different historical moments this simple script might be rephrased and expanded to address changing issues. But on the big canvas the underlying controversy between prophetic faith and civil religion emerges in bold strokes, and issues of religious liberty and church-state separation are critical. Faith must be a free response to the grace of God, translating that grace into flesh and blood, justice and kindness in all places and in every generation, in the power of the Spirit, without help or hindrance from the state.

James Dunn is a modern megaphone for that prophetic voice. And a darned good churchman, too.

— HAPPY TRAILS, JAMES DUNN — DOUG MARLETTE & REV. WILL B. DUNN

James (Dunn) and John (Leland), Baptist Sons of Zebedee

————— *Walter B. Shurden* —————

ROGER WILLIAMS AND JOHN CLARKE symbolized for Baptists in seventeenth-century America what Isaac Backus represented in the eighteenth century and John Leland embodied in the nineteenth century. And what was that? Like Amos, they stood with spines of steel in holy temples and heinous places, calling on the authorities to "let justice roll down like waters and righteousness like an ever-flowing stream" (Amos 5:24). Too little do we think of these firm friends of religious liberty as prophets.

But that's what they were. Standing for the disenfranchised and marginalized, they trumpeted the fundamental principles of fairness and freedom, both of which they rooted in the sovereignty of Almighty God. These four Baptist preachers were passionate, persistent, pietistic voices, shouting for the Baptist principle of freedom of conscience and the separation of Christ from Caesar. Like most prophets who have edged themselves into history books, they were a noisy, nagging, nettling foursome.

Without the slightest deprecation of any of the great Baptist advocates of religious freedom in the twentieth century—people such as Rufus W. Weaver, J. M. Dawson, C. Emanuel Carlson, G. Hugh Wamble, and James E. Wood, Jr.—I cast my vote for James Dunn as the one Baptist voice of twentieth-century America standing most in the train of Williams, Clarke, Backus, and Leland. And of those four, James Dunn is most like John Leland. We can with

good reason call them "James (Dunn) and John (Leland), Baptist sons of Zebedee."

You remember James and John, don't you? Jesus nicknamed these blood brothers and sons of Zebedee the "sons of Boanerges." Sons of Boanerges (Boh' uh-nuhr' jeez)! (Say it slowly several times and see if it does not remind you of Leland and Dunn.) Jesus gave his closest friends nicknames. Peter was "Rock." James and John were "Sons of Thunder," maybe "Sons of Rage." Was this a reference to their tempestuous dispositions or to their manner of speech? Were James and John the "Goldenmouths" of the apostles? We don't know.

We do know that they had fire in their souls for the cause of the Nazarene (Luke 9:54). Rustic fishermen, they left the fish and went for people (Mark 1:16-20). Along with Peter, they constituted a kitchen cabinet for Jesus. James and John were close to Christ. At the raising of Jairus' daughter (Mark 5:37), the transfiguration (Mark 9:2), and Gethsemane (Mark 14:33), they formed an inner circle of Jesus' apostles. James and John were so eager for the incoming of God's administration that one wanted to be vice-president and the other secretary of state (Mark 10:35-37). James got more than his funds cut off! He suffered martyrdom by decapitation (Acts 12:2), and John reportedly was put to death, too. James and John, biblical Sons of Thunder!

James (Dunn) and John (Leland), Baptist Sons of Thunder! Leland died in 1841 in Massachusetts. Dunn was born in 1932 in Texas. Separated by ninety-one years and two thousand miles, they are nonetheless blood brothers in many ways. I point to only four of these kinships. Both James and John are (1) heart-centered pietists, (2) freedom-loving Baptists, (3) hard-working separationists, and (4) down-home populists.

Heart-Centered Pietists

John Leland got the epitaph he requested: "Here lies the body of the Rev. John Leland, of Cheshire, who labored 67 years to promote piety and vindicate the civil and religious rights of all men."[1] Because Leland's name came to be synonymous with religious freedom and the fight for disestablishment of religion, his interpreters rush too quickly past the part of the epitaph that reads "who labored 67 years to promote piety." Piety is where you begin when you try to understand John Leland. His was a religion of the heart.

Converted under the revivalistic Separate Baptists, Leland was more concerned than anything else in life with the personal relationship between the individual and God. That was his passion, even more than religious liberty. That is what made him an itinerant evangelist. In fact, it was the inviolability of that relationship that made him a passionate advocate of religious liberty.

Also, Leland's heart-centered religion made him suspicious of theological systems. In his "Letter of Valediction on Leaving Virginia" in 1791, Leland spoke of the theological differences between Baptists in that state, especially between the Calvinists and non-Calvinists. Leland turned his pietistic card face up when he wrote:

> It is true that the schemes of both parties cannot be right; and yet both parties may be right in their aims, each wishing to justify wisdom, and make God righteous when he judgeth. He cannot be wrong, whose life and heart are right. He cannot walk amiss who walks in love. I have generally observed, that when religion is lively among the people no alienation of affection arises from a difference of judgment; and whoever considers that the Devil is orthodox in judgment, and that the Bible is not written in form of a system, will surely be moderate in dealing out hard speeches towards his heterodox brother. I conclude that the *eternal purposes* of God, and the *freedom of the human will*, are both truths; and it is a matter of fact, that the preaching that has been most blessed of God, and most profitable to men, is *the doctrine of sovereign grace in the salvation of souls, mixed with a little of what is called Arminianism.*[2]

In "The Virginia Chronicle" of 1790, one of the earliest histories of Baptists in the South, Leland reflected his disdain of theological systems, an attitude clearly rooted in his pietistic approach to matters of faith. Leland said that "it is a certain truth that the theoretic principles of men have but little effect upon their lives." He went on:

> It is no novelty in the world, for men of different sentiments, to stigmatize the doctrines of each other, with being pregnant with dangerous consequences; but it is not the doctrine or system that a man believes, that makes him either a *good* or *bad* man, but the SPIRIT he is governed by. It is a saying among lovers that "love will triumph over reason," and it is as true that the disposition of the heart will prevail over the system of the head.[3]

On the evening Leland died a young preacher visited him. Deferentially calling him "Father Leland," the young man told him that some were going to hold a prayer meeting that evening. He asked venerable old Leland, "Have you any advice to give?" Leland responded, "If you feel it in your hearts, I am glad. Forms are nothing." Said his first biographer, "He died, as he had lived, a witness for the truth, testifying, with his last breath, the value of that religion, and that only, which has its seat in the *heart*."[4]

One reason James Dunn, in his role as executive director of the Baptist Joint Committee, has worked so effectively and sympathetically with Baptists of all theological stripes is that his religion begins in his heart and not in his head. He is a heart-centered pietist, not a head-centered rationalist. In an article entitled, "Being Baptist," James (Dunn) opened with a sentence that identifies his kinship to John (Leland): "I'm a Texas-bred, Spirit-led, Bible-teaching, revival-preaching, recovering Southern Baptist."[5]

The last part of the previous sentence—"recovering Southern Baptist"—suggests Dunn has not been able to work with *all* Baptists or *all* Baptists with him. In all candor, however, the only Baptists Dunn has not been able to work with are those who forsook the historic Baptist tradition on religious liberty and those who shut out others because of their own theological rigidity. Most prominent among those Baptists were the fundamentalist leaders of Dunn's native-born Southern Baptist Convention.

It was John Leland's noncreedalistic, experiential piety and his radical commitment to religious freedom that enabled him to facilitate the union of Regular and Separate Baptists in Virginia. Likewise, it has been James Dunn's heart-felt piety and hearty love of liberty that enabled him to reach across the chasm of Baptist diversity in America and unite Baptists in the cause of freedom. No theological ideologue could ever have accomplished that. Baptists' vast theological diversity could never be led or united by either a James or a John clothed in a doctrinal straitjacket. Dunn has worked for the Baptist *Joint* Committee. His pietism facilitated the joining.

While Leland was an untheologically trained pietist, Dunn is a Ph.D. in Christian ethics whose education, solid and substantive, have pried him loose from his simple love of Jesus, his love of the church, and his commitment to fair play learned in local Baptist congregations. But let it be underscored that Dunn's piety is not a kind of superficial piosity that seeks "to substitute the devotional for the intellectual." James' piety does not consist of "superficial sloganizing." Baptists are not, says Dunn, "bibliolatrous bookworms." Rather, they are "people of the Spirit." But even that emphasis, he argues, does not reduce Baptists to antinomian subjectivists or a "navel-gazing bunch of 'touchy feelies.' "[6] Dunn's spirituality, like Leland's, is biblically and experientially rooted but void of an arrogant spirit. Heart-centered religion for James and John presupposed a broad-spirited piety that humbly allowed differences of opinion.[7]

Freedom-Loving Baptists

James and John, those witty and eccentric Baptist sons of Zebedee, are conscience-convicted, freedom-loving Baptists. While ecumenical in spirit, neither could ever be lumped into such a nondescript category as "post-denominationalists." Baptists, they believe, advocate principles that make life better for real human beings. They make no apology, therefore, for being Baptists. Leland and Dunn, so appreciative of the broad sweep of Christian history and completely aware of contributions of other Christian groups, are nevertheless pro-, not post-denominationalists. Pro-Baptists, they avoid petty sectarianism, though Leland came closer to the latter than does Dunn.

To a great degree their freedom-lovingness came from their history-awareness. Both James and John would have been wonderful church history professors, and you can bet that their classes would have been anything but boring. History walks upright for these freedom-loving kinsmen; it is passionately relevant. History, from their point of view, is a tool for activists, not something to be fondled by antique dealers. It is used to set people free, not for regurgitation on final examinations.

Leland's love of history is noted in the fact that he wrote "The Virginia Chronicle," later utilized by Robert Semple in his famous history of Baptists in Virginia. Read *The Writings of John Leland*, and you will find numerous references by this unschooled Baptist preacher to history—ancient, American, secular, and religious.

Dunn, to my knowledge, has never written history as such. But how he has used it, promoted it, and exegeted it! Back in 1991, after Supreme Court Justice Antonin Scalia had minimized the meaning of the Free Exercise Clause and Vice-President Quayle denied the significance of the No-Establishment Clause and both Democrats and Republicans in Congress were considering a five-percent cap for all charitable giving, Dunn wrote an article saying the symbol of our culture "is a digital clock which looks at only the present moment, with no hint of yesterday or tomorrow."[8] In that article Dunn plugged the importance of knowing history to preserving freedom. He said,

Perspective is essential, [one needs] a sense of history, a vision of the future, to avoid a digital clock kind of culture. It takes work to place the American experiment in context. One needs to study seriously church-state history, law, religion, public policy, and politics.9

For both James and John, being freedom-loving Baptists means vigorous anticreedalism. John Leland is famous for making one of the most quoted and quotable anticreedal statements in Baptist history. Writing in "The Virginia Chronicle," he asked of confessions of faith, "Why is this Virgin Mary between the souls of men and the Scriptures?" And then he answered:

Had a system of religion been essential to salvation, or even to the happiness of the saints, would not Jesus, who was faithful in all his house, have left us one? If he has, it is accessible to all. If he has not, why should a man be called a heretic because he cannot believe what he cannot believe, though he believes the Bible with all his heart? Confessions of faith often check any further pursuit after truth, confine the mind into a particular way of reasoning, and give rise to frequent separation. To plead for their utility, because they have been common, is as good sense as to plead for a state establishment of religion for the same reason; and both are as bad reasoning, as to plead for sin, because it is everywhere. It is sometimes said that heretics are always averse to confessions of faith. I wish I could say as much of tyrants.10

Dunn once sent me a clipping with a picture of and a quote from G. Campbell Morgan, the great English Congregationalist preacher. Morgan said, "I'm not prepared to sign any declaration drawn up by fallible human beings. I am prepared to sign, every morning and every evening and as often as it would help anyone, the whole Bible." Dunn's note to me, handwritten at the bottom of the clipping and posted to a bookshelf by my computer, says, "I thought you'd like this." He knew I would. But Dunn liked it even more than I, and that's why he sent it. He is an evangelist for anticreedalism.

With a "Lelandesque" flair to his writing, Dunn titled one of his recent "Reflections" columns as follows: "Creedless Baptists Make Tempting Targets for Legalists." Then he hammered away at the fact that Baptists have "no catechistic tests for believers." With his anticreedalism merging with his heart-centered pietism, this modern-day Leland said, "No acceptance of four or four hundred spiritual laws gets one right with God. Repentance and faith, a personal experience of God's grace—not intellectual assent to arguments—saves."[11]

Getting rhetorically airborne, Dunn argues that Baptists harbor no moral, political, or theological creed. He then notes the results of such a belief. Result number one: "Noncreedalism drives some folks *mad*." Happily pointing out that rationalism reduces religion to rules, James said, "A living faith is hard to take. It just literally drives some people crazy." Result number two: "There are true believers whom creedlessness makes *sad*." Noting that liberals are limited by scientism and fundamentalists by rationalism, Dunn went on to say that "the creed-chained character is pitiable." Result number three: "A binding creed can turn pious people *bad*," for "rigid religion," he said, "makes meanies out of otherwise decent disciples." And now to the exegesis of history: "Look at Israel, the Balkans, India, Northern Ireland, and on and on." Result number four: "A living faith not bound by creed makes Baptists *glad*."[12] And ole John Leland is leaning over the bannisters of glory, saying in that Separate Baptist whine, "Attaboy, James, sic'em; sic'em, James; sic'em."

Hard-Working Separationists

John and James pled for separation of Christ and Caesar, religion and government. Leland probably thought one could make the separation absolute. Dunn recognizes the ambiguity of the situation. Both worked tirelessly in this jungle of interconnections to avoid entanglements.

In 1776 Leland went to Virginia from his native Massachusetts. He served there as pastor and evangelist. Like brother James, a very effective preacher, John Leland spent fourteen years in the South. Again, like James a century later, he carried out his ministry in the midst of hostility from without and challenges from within Baptist circles. Leland became spokesman for the General Committee of Baptists, surely one of the earliest expressions of the later Baptist Joint Committee on Public Affairs. Leland and Virginia Baptists are given much of the credit for the ratification of the Federal Constitution and the later adoption of the Bill of Rights. Leland worked so hard to separate religion and government that some called him the "political parson." Dunn has shared similar titles.

Toleration was not the goal for John; nor has it been an ideal for James. Because some in his day thought that state churches and religious toleration could be reconciled, Leland, writing with pen on fire, said, "The very tendency of religious establishments by human law is to make some hypocrites and the rest fools." He continued:

> Government should protect every man in thinking and speaking freely, and see that one does not abuse another. The liberty I contend for is more than toleration. The very idea of toleration is despicable; it supposes that some have a preeminence above the rest to grant indulgence; whereas all should be equally free, Jews, Turks, Pagans, and Christians.[13]

In one of his most forceful essays Leland said that "government has no more to do with the religious opinions of men than it has with the principles of mathematics." And then this freedom-loving separationist of church and state said, "Let every man speak freely without fear, maintain the principles that he believes, worship according to his own faith, either one God, three Gods, no God, or twenty Gods; and let government protect him in so doing."[14]

James, following in the footsteps of brother John, sees clearly the political corollary of the theological principle of soul freedom. It is separation of religion and government. But Dunn is also clear that "separation of church and state" does not mean separation of God from government or Christians from citizenship. He also recognizes that separation is "messy, difficult, inconsistent." But if it is not neat, neither is it obsolete, for "when government meddles in religion it always has the touch of mud." Moreover, Dunn acknowledges that the separation for which he has labored is not a "complete" separation of church and state. While there may not be a "wall of separation" between the two, there must remain a distinction and a distance. If not a "wall," says Dunn, we must at least have a "strand of 'barbed wire.'"[15]

One should not leave the work of James and John on the separation of church and state without noting one significant fact. Their political activism stems primarily from their religious pietism; not, as some would contend, from Enlightenment rationalism. Because God is Lord of the conscience and because individuals must answer to God alone, the soul must be free from coercion of all kinds, including a coercive state. Authentic pietism, rooted in a transforming spirituality, gave rise to the cry for religious freedom and the corresponding insistence on separation of church and state.

Down-Home Populists

Neither John Leland nor James Dunn was into personal image making. To the contrary, they must be seen as folksy, unpretentious, "aw-shucks" kinds of Baptist preachers. While the ordinary people heard them gladly because of their common touch, James and John each walked in some rather high cotton, hobnobbing with some of the most powerful and influential people in the nation. Neither, one senses, came away from such gatherings over-impressed with himself or with the prominent and powerful.

These Baptist brothers of Zebedee stand in a grand tradition of Baptist popularizers. To use preacher language of Leland and Dunn, "They were good on their feet." In his classic history of Baptists in Virginia, Robert B. Semple said of John Leland: "Leland, as a preacher, was probably the most popular of any that ever resided in this state. He is unquestionably a man of fertile genius."16

Similar words could be uttered about James Dunn. I have never asked him, but I would be willing to wager that if you asked him to describe himself, he would say something like, "I am a Baptist preacher." Tapped for the leadership of the Baptist Joint Committee on Public Affairs because of his intellectual acumen, social savvy, and commitment to Baptist ideals, Dunn is essentially a Texas Baptist, called of God to preach the gospel. If you scratch him, and you will not have to scratch deeply, you will find a down-home Baptist preacher who believes supremely in the grace of God for sinful souls.

Leland and Dunn have spontaneity in common. But make no mistake about it. Before they said what they said or wrote what they wrote, they had thought long and hard about the best way to say or write it, so the average person could get it. And they did it with a razor sharp wit and creative language. Speaking of the Presbyterians and their effort to make New Testament baptism analogous to Old Testament circumcision, Leland said, "I could not, for my gizzard, understand their *orthography*, until I was more than sixteen. They would spell thus: c-i-r, cir, c-u-m, cum, c-i, ci, s-e-d, *baptism*."17

Preachers would do well to study Dunn's "Reflections" columns in *Report from the Capital* to learn how to write for both the ear and the eye. Truncated, pithy, conversation-like sentences, followed by a meandering, snake-like sentence, give rhythm and cadence to his writing and speaking. Beneath the rhythm of the words lies a substantial but unobtrusive theology. I illustrate with an article he wrote in 1998 on campaign finance reform as a moral issue. Note both the profound theology and the down-home style:

Two universals should concern us. One is the dignity that should be afforded to every human being made in the image of God. The other is the fallibility of all humankind. Even when we know what's right, understand the difference between good and evil, and appreciate the course of action that serves our own interests, we blow it. And that's even more true of special interests. When we band together it's worse: in Niebuhr's words, "moral man and immoral society."

And so, political parties, corporations, wealthy individuals, sleazy publications, big contributors, industries, businessmen, labor unions, moneyed interests, and even justices of the Supreme Court can see money as having absolute rights of free speech. "If God says, lovin' money is the root of all sin, then God is unAmerikin."

Of course, contributions affect votes in Congress. How stupid do they think we are? Campaign finance reform is a moral issue.[18]

As I said earlier, James and John, the biblical sons of Zebedee, spent time with Jesus. So did the Baptists James and John. As a result, they spoke creatively, imaginatively, and straightforwardly.

Conclusion

Leland's nineteenth-century legacy of "promoting piety and vindicating the civil and religious rights of all" is the baton he picked up from Roger Williams, John Clarke, and Isaac Backus. Likewise, it is James Dunn's twentieth-century gift to Baptists in particular and American citizens in general. Now with the retirement of Dunn as executive director of the Baptist Joint Committee on Public Affairs, the question looms really huge for Baptists and the future of freedom in America, "Who will pick up the baton for Baptists in the twenty-first century?"

Notes

[1] *The Writings of John Leland*, ed. L. F. Greene (New York: Arno Press, 1969) 50.

[2] Ibid., 172. Compare Leland's statement on Calvinism and Arminianism to the following brief paragraph by Dunn. "We live with competing values, principles that must be held paradoxically, goods that complement rather than contradict. You may think of God's providential foreordination and the concept of free moral agency. The dynamic dyads abound. They hit us every day, and not just in seminaries." See James M. Dunn, "Being Baptist," in *Baptists in the Balance*, ed. Everett C. Goodwin (Valley Forge PA: Judson Press, 1997) 219.

[3] Ibid., 111.

[4] Ibid., 49.

[5] Dunn, "Being Baptist," 219.

[6] Ibid., 223. See this reference for all quotes in this paragraph.

[7] For an elaboration on Dunn's idea that Baptists should have enough humility to permit differences of opinion, see his "Being Baptist," 225-26. His experiential pietism is the root of his anticocksureness. "More important and satisfying than answers," he says, "is The Answer." And then he adds, "Thou are with me—that's what we crave."

[8] James M. Dunn, "Reflections," *Report from the Capital*, 46/2 (February 1991): 15.

[9] Ibid.

[10] *The Writings of John Leland*, 114. See also pp. 39, 50, and 51.

[11] James M. Dunn, "Reflections: Creedless Baptists Make Tempting Targets for Legalists," *Report from the Capital*, 54/5 (9 March 1999): 3.

[12] Ibid.

[13] *The Writings of John Leland*, 118.

[14] Ibid., 184.

[15] James M. Dunn, "The Baptist Vision of Religious Liberty," ed. Walter B. Shurden, *Proclaiming the Baptist Vision: Religious Liberty* (Macon GA: Smyth & Helwys Publishing, Inc, 1997) 36.

[16] Robert B. Semple, *A History of the Rise and Progress of the Baptists in Virginia* (Richmond VA: Published by the author, 1810) 158. What Leland's first biographer said of him could as easily be said of James Dunn: "The great object, (next in importance to his mission as a preacher of Christ), for which he seems to have been raised up by a special Providence, was to promote the establishment of religious liberty in the United States." See *The Writings of John Leland*, 52.

17*The Writings of John Leland,* 73.

18James M. Dunn, "Reflections: Personal Freedom Has Stake in Campaign Finance Reform," *Report from the Capital,* 53/10 (19 May 1998): 3.

Contributors

Lynn A. Bergfalk has served as senior minister of Calvary Baptist Church in Washington, D.C., for the past twelve years. He is a graduate of Yale Divinity School and holds the D.Min. from Wesley Theological Seminary.

Tony Campolo is an ordained Baptist minister and professor of sociology at Eastern College in St. Davids, Pennsylvania. He is a well-known speaker/lecturer and the author of more than ten books, including *Carpe Diem*; *It's Friday, But Sunday's Coming*; *The Kingdom of God Is a Party*; *20 Hot Potatoes Christians Are Afraid To Touch*; and *How To Be Pentecostal Without Speaking in Tongues*.

Marvin C. Griffin has served as pastor of Ebenezer Baptist Church in Austin, Texas, since 1969 and as adjunct professor of pastoral ministry at Southwestern Baptist Theological Seminary since 1992. He is a former chair of the board of the Baptist Joint Committee and former first vice-president of the Baptist General Association of Texas.

Mark O. Hatfield served as a U.S. Senator for thirty years. Earlier he held public office in the state of Oregon, including two terms as governor. He now lectures in several colleges, chairs a biomedical research funding iniative, and fills a 1998 presidential appointment to the National Institutes of Health National Advisory Council on Aging.

John Newport is special consultant for academic research and adjunct professor at Southwestern Baptist Theological Seminary, having retired as vice-president for academic affairs and provost. He is distinguished professor of philosophy of religion, emeritus. He has also served as a professor at Baylor University, New Orleans Baptist Seminary, and Rice University.

Pam Parry was congressional correspondent for Baptist News Service and associate director of communications for the Baptist Joint Committee from 1991 to 1996. She has since served as adjunct lecturer for American University and George Washington University's Center for Career Education. She recently joined the faculty of Taylor University, Upland, Indiana, as assistant professor of communication arts.

A. James Rudin is the National Interreligious Affairs Director of the American Jewish Committee. He is a proud former member of Boy Scout Troop 131, which met at First Baptist Church in Alexandria, Virginia.

Walter B. Shurden is Callaway Professor of Christianity and chair of the department of Christianity at Mercer University, Macon, Georgia. He is the author and editor of numerous works on Baptist history.

Michael Smith resides in Washington, D.C., and is employed by the Florence Fund. He is a native of Missouri, where he attended William Jewell College and the University of Missouri.

Oliver S. Thomas is a former general counsel of the Baptist Joint Committee. He now serves as special counsel to the National Council of Churches and to the First Amendment Center at Vanderbilt University.

Victor Tupitza served American Baptist Churches, USA, as a pastor in Philadelphia and in the division of communications. He is former editor of *Report from the Capital* and of *Capital Baptist*, a publication of the District of Columbia Baptist Convention.

Foy Valentine has served in numerous denominational and national capacities in support of applied Christianity initiatives. Among these are his current presidency of the Center for Chrisitian Ethics in Dallas, Texas. He is former executive director of the Christian Life Commission of the Southern Baptist Convention and of the Texas Baptist Christian Life Commission.